WHEN FEAR
IS NOT AN OPTION

You Can't Run Away from Your Feet

David Doctor

2-3-2014

BALBOA.
PRESS
A DIVISION OF HAY HOUSE

Balboa Press books may be ordered through booksellers or by contacting:

Balboa Press
A Division of Hay House
1663 Liberty Drive
Bloomington, IN 47403
www.balboapress.com
1 (877) 407-4847

Because of the dynamic nature of the Internet, any web addresses or links contained in this book may have changed since publication and may no longer be valid. The views expressed in this work are solely those of the author and do not necessarily reflect the views of the publisher, and the publisher hereby disclaims any responsibility for them.

The author of this book does not dispense medical advice or prescribe the use of any technique as a form of treatment for physical, emotional, or medical problems without the advice of a physician, either directly or indirectly. The intent of the author is only to offer information of a general nature to help you in your quest for emotional and spiritual well-being. In the event you use any of the information in this book for yourself, which is your constitutional right, the author and the publisher assume no responsibility for your actions.

Any people depicted in stock imagery provided by Thinkstock are models, and such images are being used for illustrative purposes only. Certain stock imagery © Thinkstock.

Printed in the United States of America.

ISBN: 978-1-4525-8686-1 (sc)
ISBN: 978-1-4525-8688-5 (hc)
ISBN: 978-1-4525-8687-8 (e)

Balboa Press rev. date: 12/04/2013

To my father, Roy Doctor, who taught me about responsibility, determination, and family values, and to my mother, Jeanette Doctor, who has always believed in me and been an inspiration to me to do better and to be the best person I can be.

CONTENTS

INTRODUCTION

FEAR—we all fear *something* in our life! Many of us have a lot of fears about the future, the unknowns in life, traveling, or about our country's future. Fear can control us or we can control it, but how do people control their fears?

When the economy is going crazy; when you have lost your job and do not know how to pay your mortgage; when animals and insects put chills up your spine; when you are scared about retirement; when you don't know whether to buy a house or rent; when you are scared of water, heights, small places, big crowds of people, or even clowns; when fears stop you in your tracks and cause you to panic and run away; when fear is so strong that you cannot think rationally, speak coherently, or control bodily functions—when fear controls you—and when you know other people do not feel this way and you do not know how to overcome this fear—life can seem like an insurmountable challenge. Your fears can be devastating to your life and career.

If you're paralyzed by fears, you know you must turn the situation around, but how do you do this? The author Neale Donald Walsch said, "FEAR is an acronym in the English language for 'False Evidence Appearing Real.'" So how do you deal with fear being false evidence? How do you see the truth, that there is nothing to fear, and that the "evidence" you see is not real? In this book we will look into fear—the symptoms—and then the strategies you can use to overcome your fears and help others.

If you decide to face your fears, and you walk up to that wall of fear and push yourself to go beyond it no matter what the inner voice and self-talk may say, you will not be disappointed.

It will take a lot of strength, willpower, self-control, and practice, but once you unlock those capabilities in yourself you will have a greater insight into your own psychological makeup and you'll be in a good position to create a plan to fulfill your dreams.

Everyone who has faced a fear in his or her life has faced a wall of fear, various boundaries beyond which he or she was afraid to venture. This book is not about whether you have fears, because we all do. It is about *what you do* when your fears present an obstacle to you in your life. What do you do then? What do you say to yourself? What does your physical body do now when fear strikes? Do you run from the fear or face the fear?

Can you relate to fear and go beyond it? Do you see fear as a wall that you cannot pass through? Or is the wall a challenge for you—a challenge to find a door or window to get through, or a challenge to find a way to scale to the top and get over the wall?

The question I hear people ask most about conquering fear is, "How? How do I do it? What steps can I take to overcome these fears?" In the following pages we will address these questions and find ways to break the wall into small pieces so the rubble can be scaled.

We'll look at various points in the life of Mark, who suffered from the kind of fear that paralyzes a person. We'll look at how he did conquer his fear, and we'll look at the influences in his life that made it possible for him to scale his rather high wall of fear.

CHAPTER 1

---◈══◈---

MARK'S FEAR

In life all people face hard times. They have fears about the future, about losing their jobs, their homes, their families, and their health.

As an individual, you may feel like your problems and fears are all yours, and you may feel all alone. Your thoughts are focused inward, and the fear consumes your time. You are seeking a way out, an open door, a way to find more money, more security, more help, more compassion, and more reassurance. You are hoping the feelings will pass and the fear will go away.

Your life may feel like a giant vacuum cleaner has sucked your dreams, your life, and your confidence away. Fear can make things look hopeless; fear can freeze you in your tracks. Mark's fear scared him so much that he was frozen and not able to run or fight for his own life. The question was and always will be whether he was tougher than the fear.

Whenever Mark smelled chlorine in a swimming pool or bleach when doing laundry he was transported back to when he was just 10 years old and taking swimming lessons. He remembered standing on the edge of the high school's Olympic-sized pool, wanting to run away but too obedient to move. He felt the extreme anxiety, the raw, knee-shaking fear and the panic of entering the water. He wondered if those feelings would ever go away. Mark was thinking of the time when he was a young Boy Scout taking swim classes for his First Class merit badge.

He remembered standing in line on the side of the pool, shaking from cold (but mainly from the intense fear) and hoping something would happen to stop, delay, or end the pool session early. Can fear so occupy the mind that a person cannot function logically, focus on learning something new, or ultimately save his own life? He thought, "What have I done to deserve this water torture?" Would he drown today? Would he drink chlorine water and swallow air until his stomach was full? What would he do if he could not swim to the side of the pool? Would a hand be there when he would need it?

"The bravest sight in the world is to see a great man struggling against adversity." – Lucius Annaeus Seneca

---

What kind of torture must he endure? Would he continue burping chlorine from swallowing air and water? He thought, "God, what have I done to deserve this water torture?"

Mark was trying to listen to the instructions but didn't believe what they were saying. All Mark was thinking was that he was only 3 ft. 8 in. tall and the shallow part of the pool was four feet deep. The water was over his head, and he could not breathe water. *Who would save me if I get in trouble?* His mother and father always took care of him, but they were not there to save him if he had a problem. Fear occupied Mark's mind so much that he was not able to rationally think of a solution or to apply the concepts that the swimming instructors were teaching. Mark was being controlled by his fear, and he was losing the battle for his mind. Why does fear stop a person from listening to reason, or from overcoming his or her fears and seeing a clear solution?

Mark needed to pass swimming lessons to earn the First Class merit badge for the Boy Scouts. His father and mother put him in the swimming classes and expected him to pass. He was from a big family, and the money for these classes was hard to come by. Mark was scared out of his wits, but fear held him back from believing he could learn to swim.

Mark was a quiet and shy child, and he would not have said he was scared (male pride, possibly), and he was raised in a time when you did not disobey your parents, elders, or other adults. It is not clear why Mark was afraid of the water; there was no traumatic event to cause the fear. Maybe it was the fear of the unknown, or fear of failure, or a lack of confidence in the water.

Mark was enrolled in the swimming class to pass it, not to waste time or money. He wanted to be a success and make everyone happy, but fear had a hold on him and he just wanted to go home. Yes, this was Mark's thinking.

No matter what was going on inside Mark's mind, he tried to act as if things were great. He tried to make people believe he was happy and then say what he thought they wanted to hear, while deep inside he was thinking, "What the hell am I doing here?" Mark was shaking like a leaf in the wind—he was cold, the pool was big, and the water was deep with that nasty smell of chlorine permeating the entire pool area.

Mark was very content to be in a room of people and say nothing. Talking was not important, and to speak in a crowd of people was extremely stressful and one of the most scary things to contemplate doing. Mark did not need to verbalize his thoughts to come to a conclusion; he was able to process internally, analyze a situation, and find a workable solution. His grandfather once said, "He wouldn't say shit if he had a mouthful." Mark was a quiet child and was content to be a spectator and not a participant in the pool. He feared the pool, the chlorine water, and the deep water that was over his head.

You may ask why Mark didn't say anything. Why didn't he speak? Why do most scared people hold their tongues? Well, in most cases, people will not speak because they do not feel safe! Something inside tells them, "If I speak they will laugh," or they might say, "You are wrong."

They might add, "What are you thinking? Tell me."

Fear can also render a person speechless, so maybe that was the case with Mark.

If your spouse, fiancé or fiancée, or boyfriend or girlfriend does not speak, maybe he or she does not feel safe. Fear makes people quiet.

Why? Because they do not feel safe saying what they think—they are scared. Mark was no different. He did not feel safe and he was scared.

That's why people say:

> "It scared the heck out of him."
> "He was so scared his boots at home were shaking."
> "She was so scared she couldn't speak."
> "It scared the crap out of him."
> "He was so scared, his grandma's teeth were chattering."
> "He was white as a sheet."
> "He was so scared he couldn't move."
> "She was scared out of her wits."
> "He was as nervous as a cat on hot bricks."
> "She was scared of her own shadow."

Can fear so occupy your thoughts that you will not act, you will not listen to reason, and you will not trust others who say, "You can do it!"? Can fear hold you back from learning, performing, and trying? Can fear consume your rational thinking? Can fear stop you from being a success, even when you say you want to succeed? Can fear stop you from fighting and speaking out for a good cause? Can fear stop you from getting involved? Can fear hold you back from speaking out for a just cause? Can fear of outside forces in the culture, like peer pressure, political correctness, and keeping up with the Joneses, hold you back from speaking and defending what is right? How many times have you said, "I should have spoken up, I should've said something"? Can fear of life's situations and challenges allow you to think that suicide is the only answer? Can fear cause you to expect a government handout instead of risking and working hard to secure a future where you can hold your head high and be proud of your accomplishments? Can fear hold you back from speaking until things get so bad that you have no choice but to speak out?

Was Mark the only person who was scared of the water? Looking at the other children who jumped in and swam easily, Mark thought it must be a personal problem. Was he the only child struggling with this fear? Were the other children stronger inside, or did they not have this fear? Mark did not know why the other children were successful, why they were not afraid, why they did as they were told and made it look so easy. He was paralyzed by the fear, and the other children were not. Why is one person struck with fear and scared of dogs and others walk by as if they are not? Why is it that boys pick up frogs, lizards, and bugs, but most girls are terrified of them? The bug reacts the same to the boys and the girls, but there is a different perception of that situation. Where does the fear come from, and why does the fear produce such an emotional response?

Mark thought that the logical answer was that he must be an oddball, a sissy, and a loser. Just because you have a fear of something, are you different, a freak, or an oddball? Do all people fear something? Do lots of people fear spiders, snakes, the dark, confined spaces, closets, clowns, failure, speaking in front of a crowd, and death? Mark felt that he was not normal for having his fear of the water. He felt that since others were not scared, he should not be scared. Was it a deficiency in him? Was he a mouse and not a man? What was it? It seems that people who have a fear of something will try to hide it, not talk about it, and hope it goes away, but it *will not* go away by itself—it is a part of them, like a lung or a kidney. The question is whether one can overcome the fear.

Mark did not talk about this fear—he tried to avoid it, ignore it, and stay away from the water. Why is it that fear holds a person back from being all he can be? Is it part of life's equation that in order to have success in anything, there is a price to pay, and that price might be pain, challenges, and fear?

Those who have fear think they are in some way deficient, lacking something that others have. They may feel that they are a loser, incomplete, and lacking self-confidence in a particular situation. Fear is a real roadblock for them. It is so large that it may as well be the Grand Canyon that they cannot get across. For some, it may seem like a brick wall 33 feet tall and 27 feet thick, with no doors or windows, a wall that is impossible to scale, like the Great Wall of China, which is designed to keep you out. For them this fear is impassable; of course, it looks illogical to the casual observer, but it is very real to the person who experiences raw fear.

People who fear success will get right to the finish line—and then everything falls apart. They will freeze up, forget their lines, become physically exhausted, lose coordination, or lose their self-confidence and motivation to continue. People, who fear success will quit, give up on their dreams, stop short of achieving their goals, and neglect to follow through on their desires. It's not that they do not want success—it's just impossible for them to see a road to get them there.

Some people have a fear of losing, and they have a head as big as the cartoon character Fred Flintstone, with an ego that doesn't let them lose in any situation. This fear of losing coupled with poor ethics and moral values can cause them to lie, cheat, gossip, and point the finger of blame at others. They think in their mind that they are always right, always doing the right things, and what they do is cooler than what anyone else does. They will put others down so they will look better to others and in their own mind. They are hard to talk to and do not listen to leaders, bosses, or others, even if they are in the wrong. They can be damaging to a team's morale, they can sabotage a team's good plan for their own personal gain, and they can blame failures on other members of the team. They do not even see this fear as fear—they see it as a driving force that makes them successful and great in their own mind. They are their best cheerleader and fan club members. The fear of losing will motivate them to cheat to make themselves a winner and others the losers.

Fear has a person believing that the thing they are afraid of is truly dangerous to them, and the fear then controls the person's thinking. Then strong feelings of fear become their reality, and they believe that the feared thing is really lethal and that they cannot get past it. However, this is not really the case, or the truth. It's a case of "False Evidence Appearing Real."

Mark, a fifth-grader at the time, wanted to complete the swimming course, but he had a large list of reasons why he could not do this. He was shy and scared of putting his face under the water. The instructors taught him how to get a breath, but he was afraid of sinking and not being able to pull himself up to the surface or how to swim up to the surface. He had a fear of not getting air, which clouded all common-sense thinking. Of course, he was also too short, and the water was way over his head. He didn't know the instructors and didn't trust them to give him a hand when he had a can't-reach-the-side-of-the-pool problem; the water was too cold; he was smaller than the other kids; the pool was too deep; and the pool was too big.

He had plenty of good excuses and lots of wild excuses. Of course, he had a solution, and that was to go home—*that would solve the whole problem*—just run away and not face the pool and swim class.

Most people are just like Mark. They have many excuses and reasons why they do not go beyond their fears and accomplish their dreams in life.

Mark's fear dominated his conscious mind so completely that he was not physically able to swim. When he jumped in the water he was so scared that the idea of moving his arms and legs was overruled by the thought of grabbing for the side of the pool. Mark's dominating thought was the security of holding on to the side of the pool.

Mark saw the water in the pool as a big entity that would engulf him and not allow him to get air. It would grab him and hold him down, and he felt that he would not be able to overcome the water and get to the air that he desperately needed for life. He believed that holding on to the side of the pool was his only way to feel safe; swimming over an arm's length from the side was outside his comfort zone. The open water embodied the wall of fear for Mark.

His security was to hold the side of the pool and pull himself out when he needed air. Mark did not understand physics, water displacement, buoyancy, hydrodynamics, or the strokes needed to get him from the bottom of the pool to the surface. All he knew was that the wall of fear was great and that he could not break through it. He knew if he could reach the side of the pool he was going to be able to get air when he needed it. Any further than an arm's length from the side of the pool was a wall he could not get past.

Mark stood there watching the other students swim. You would think that Mark would have faith and believe the strokes that they took would work for him. But as it is with all fears, one is incapable of seeing another person's successes and then copying what they did. Even though Mark was taught how to do the strokes and he saw others have success doing them, he couldn't get past his fear and do as they did or as the instructors taught him. He did not have faith that he could do it. Fear does not work on the rational part of the mind.

When a soldier in battle charges the enemy, there are some that see that move not as the means to victory but as the means to defeat and death. That is why we have heroes in battle and medals of Honor awarded. Their belief in their success was stronger than their fear of what might happen, and they moved forward even when they were scared. When someone is scared and you tell them it is okay and that there is nothing to fear, they do not believe you. They do not see it as you see it, and they may even become hysterical and need you to slap them in the face to get their attention. Fear is telling them to act—there is no time to analyze the situation, so their fear either makes them move toward what they fear or away from what they fear and to a safe place. This is known as the "fight-or-flight response."

Mark did not have enough information and confidence to face the deep water; he always wanted to take flight to a safe place (the side of the pool).

Belief is *not* a part of the equation when you have fear. In fact, they seem to be opposites. People who are scared usually react first, run, scream or freeze in their tracks. They do not stop and evaluate their faith and belief in the situation. Only when they decide to overcome their fear do they think about their level of belief that they can do it. Some Christians fear they will not get to heaven. When they have this fear, it blocks out their belief, which is so vital for Christians because they believe in things that are not seen. They have the faith to overcome fears of rejection, persecution and even death.

At the end of the first swimming class, Mark could not swim a single stroke with his face in the water. He could swim the sidestroke, sort of, and could dog paddle, but he had no faith that this method of "swimming" would work for long, probably only long enough to get him to the side of the pool. He was a bundle of nerves and was too scared to even think of asking to quit swimming lessons.

Mark's accomplishment was to go underwater while he held on to the side of the pool for security. He could also hold on to a floating device and leave the side of the pool. These were his only personal achievements in swimming class that first year and it was not good enough for him to pass swimming in the Boy Scouts.

The next year he was enrolled for swimming classes for the second time. Now he was doomed to relive the fears of the first year. The only real feeling he had was that of being a loser. He did not understand why he could not swim like the other children or what he needed to do differently, so he felt he was doomed to react the same way as he had the previous year. If you keep doing what you're doing, you'll keep getting what you are getting. And Mark was full of fear and repeated what he learned the first year. He held on to the side of the pool and shook like a cat crapping razor blades. He jumped in and swam to the safety of the side of the pool. However, this was not swimming, and as in most learning, the slow learners fall by the wayside.

"Fear makes come true that which one is afraid of." – Victor Frankl

---

Have you ever been so scared that you cannot think straight, no matter how many people said there was nothing to fear, or that being scared was stupid? Have you ever been called on in school to answer a question and just gone blank, even when you know the answer?

They say all the world is a stage—well, when the curtain opens, the actor emerges and recites the lines practiced, and the only lines Mark knew meant failure. Mark knew how to hit the water and gasp for air, he knew how to open his eyes wide with fear, he understood the panic that goes through the mind of a cat when you try to give them their first bath. He knew the look, hair all wet and stuck to their small body, eyes as big as a frog's eyes, all claws bared and hanging on to the side of the sink with all their legs spread and whining and yowling.

Mark knew how to shiver and get to the back of the line and to hold on to the ladder and lean forward but not go anywhere because fear wouldn't let him let go. Fear was part of the character that he was playing. What could he do to change the actor or to change the script? Mark just listened to the inner voice that guided him. Unfortunately, the voice kept saying, "Stay calm, don't get panicky, RUN FOR YOUR LIFE!" Of course, he blocked out the voice that told him to run away. He did this because he *had* to do what the adult instructors told him to do, and he had to go to swimming classes. However, the voice kept saying to run home, get to the side of the pool, save yourself. Mark did not know how to get past this dilemma, or how to pass the swim test. He knew that to pass the swim test he would first have to get through, around, or over this wall of fear that was between him and the final swim test. However, this wall was too big for him. There were no visible doors to go through or a ladder to climb. Mark was never taught how to face this fear, to never quit, to persevere, to move toward what you fear and not away from it. He also did not know why it was a good idea to learn to swim, and why he should do it. He needed a good plan, but all he had was last year's plan.

His plan was to jump in the water, reach for the side, and get out fast—yeah! *That's the ticket*, he told himself.

Of course, getting away from the thing you fear doesn't solve anything, but to an 11-year-old kid it seemed right.

One day in swim class the entire class was told to line up at the ladder. Each student, while holding on, was to step down on the first rung of the ladder, push off, and swim to the other side of the pool. When it was Mark's turn, he climbed down. He was told to push off from the ladder and swim. *What? I can't do that.* But he knew he must try. He held on to the ladder and every muscle in his body said *don't go*. He hesitated, leaned forward to push off, and then pulled back to the ladder. Then he leaned forward again. The instructor said, "Get in the water, you're holding everyone back." Again he leaned forward, pushed off, but then pulled back to the ladder. His feet were ready to go, but his hand would not let go. Mark finally pushed off, but one hand would not let go, he spun around, left the ladder went out about two feet and sunk under water. Mark thought, *Oh shoot! Now what?*

He pushed off the bottom to get to the surface. All Mark wanted was to get some air; there was no rational thinking about trying to swim, or dog paddle—all he wanted was air and the security of the side of the pool. He repeatedly reached for the side, but the side of the pool was a foot out of his reach.

Panic was his only friend and he embraced his friend with all his might. He reached for the side, stood on his tiptoes, and drank mouthfuls of water. Mark was bobbing like a cork and could not get closer to the side of the pool or get a full breath of air without water. As his eyes broke the surface they were as big as two duck eggs and bulging out of their sockets. He looked for help, but the other kids were in line waiting for Mark to get out of the way. As he went under, all sounds deafened and were muffled. All Mark could hear was his heartbeat and the swishing of water. Mark was not crying for help; he was saving all his energy to get another bit of air. Mark was in a world of his own. Every thought was survival—every thought was to find the side of the pool—but all he could grab was water, water, and more water. After bobbing for what seemed like 20 minutes, someone grabbed him by the arm. It was the instructor, and Mark was pulled to the side of the pool and severely reprimanded.

The instructor said, "Quit goofing off, and get out of the pool. You are wasting all of our time." Mark held on to the side of the pool for dear life, while thinking, *GOOFING OFF? Is goofing off and drowning the same thing?*

Mark almost drowned, drank a lot of pool water, could not get to the surface for air—his eyes were the size of golf balls—and panic was his only thought, and now he was reprimanded for wasting the instructor's time and other students' time, and to stop goofing off in the water. *WOW!* Mark thought that he may be the slow kid that is holding the rest of the class back, but what if he had drowned? That would really hold the class back. So now his new dilemma was, do you drown or goof off? Both are bad for the class, but both would be very bad for Mark.

All he could think was, *I almost drowned, and now I am in trouble for wasting others' time. And the instructor is pissed at me. Would he ever help me again? Maybe the next time I will drown and how awful of a feeling that would be!* Mark knew he didn't want to wake up dead on the bottom of the pool, if that was even possible.

Should he trust the instructor to help, and will the instructor teach him how to go beyond this fear and have the confidence to continue to learn, practice, and have the small successes that could help to move him forward? Mark didn't know about positive thinking, positive affirmations, mind over matter, goal setting, habits of highly successful people, or a goal-driven life. He was only thinking of survival and not drowning. Self-preservation was at the top of his list of priorities, and running away was what he wanted to do. Mark was on the bottom of Maslow's hierarchy of needs and didn't even know who Maslow was. Mark wanted air, and he thought he could not go underwater for fear of not having air. Those who fear dogs, snakes, spiders, or any animal fear being bitten more than anything. And rationally thinking that the dog may be nice, just as the owner says, that the animal is more scared of you, doesn't occur to these people. Words of reassurance have no meaning to the person with fear.

Unfortunately, despite all the instruction he received, Mark didn't learn to swim or find the confidence in the water. He was still scared of the deep water and needed the security of the side of the pool and the security of a floating device. *Will he always stay in the shallow end of the pool? Will he always jump in and swim from the ladder to the side, and hold on to the side for security? Would he be destined to use a kick board (for security) to swim across the pool?* These were the questions he asked himself.

Well, Mark never passed the First Class level in the Boy Scouts, because if you cannot swim, then you cannot sign off that level. This failure led to a desire to quit the Boy Scout program altogether. And of course Mark did quit the Boy Scouts and never completed the swim lessons or that level in the Scouts. He was actually relieved that he would not have to face the pool again.

When you get away from the thing you fear, the fear goes away temporarily. Mark knew that as long as he stayed away from swimming lessons he would never be forced to get into the water again. No one would ever put him into a swimming program, and this fear would be over forever. And as time passed he got bigger, and smarter, and believed he could go through life and avoid the whole swimming issue. This was a good plan, he thought, and his only plan.

However, God had other plans for Mark.

It is said: "If you want God to laugh, tell him your plans."

Mark avoided the water and avoided swimming every chance he got. He would even, on summer vacations, sit on the side of the pool or in the shallow end of the pool and tell others, like his little sister, how to swim. This way he would avoid actually putting his head underwater, and he was able to stay in his comfort zone.

CHAPTER 2

MARK IS THE PINBALL

When Mark started kindergarten, he was only four years old because his birthday came after the September start of school. He became five in kindergarten, so he was younger than most of the children in his class and of course was always a year behind in size.

Mark was the runt of the boys in his class and was teased about his size. They would ask him, "Where did you get your clothes, from GI Joe?" They would say, "Mark stand up—Oh! You *are* standing up." When he played sports he was a year behind the other kids and had to put out more effort for the same performance. He had to try harder playing games at recess and try harder on tests—even the girls were bigger than he was. Mark was smaller until his junior and senior years, when the others stopped growing and Mark caught up with his classmates. This gave him a bit more self-esteem, but he still saw himself as smaller than others. He also was accustomed to putting out more effort, trying harder in sports at gym class, and hanging to the back of the crowd. When Mark was in his senior year in high school he knew he would graduate at the early age of 17, young, dumb, and with no job experience. What would he do?

One day in school they announced that all seniors who wanted to take the military entrance exam needed to go to the cafeteria. Of course, Mark was not interested in fighting or the military, but once they said you will be there all morning for testing and you will be excused from class, that was his ticket to get out of class. So Mark and his friends all went to take this stupid test that they could not fail, and of course "getting out of class" were the magic words. Little did they know that this was a good tool for the recruiters. They collected test scores, picked the best candidates, and they had your names and addresses for future contacts. This was a seed planted in the minds of young people. The military provided food, lodging, clothes (uniforms), training, education, and best of all, it got you away from home and out of the hometown thinking. Like they say, "Join the Army and see the Navy. Join the Navy and see the world."

While in high school, Mark and his buddies saw *American Graffiti*, a movie about the 1950s and life in a small town. In the movie, some were going off to college, and some kids loved their town and were not willing to leave and were even scared to leave. Mark related to the movie and the decision to move on, but he did not have a scholarship, a job, a car, or any plan for his future. Was he destined to work in the steel mills, factories, or the hometown businesses? Mark and his buddies copied the movie and were accustomed to cruising "the strip," a term for driving the car around the three major streets in town looking for action (as if Mark would know what to do with "action" if he found it). So one day Mark and his best friend were driving the strip and they decided to go to the big city of Hammond, Indiana. This was a big road trip and a bit more exciting than cruising the strip in Griffith, Indiana. They drove down the main street past the historic homes, closed factories, and the military recruiters with their big signs and cool posters for joining the military and going to Vietnam.

They remembered the test they took months ago and were curious about how they scored, so Mark made a decision with his best friend to go see the recruiters and see what kind of a deal they could get. So they made a U-turn and went to see what kind of a line of crap they would be fed. First they went to the Army recruiter (no swimming required). The Army recruiter seemed rough and tough but lacked simple common sense. He thought going to Vietnam, fighting for his country, and getting shot at was exciting. He also couldn't pronounce certain words, such as "pencil." He also said "niner" not "nine." Crazy—Mark and his buddy didn't want to die for their country in Vietnam, so they went to see the Marine recruiter.

When they entered the office, they saw that the Marine recruiter had all his hair cut off, had sharp creases on his uniform trousers, and had shoes so shiny that you could see your face in them. There was more discipline in this guy's pinky than in their whole body. They thought the Army guy was crazy but that this Marine guy was "Who rah!" A real America-loving, spit-shined, wanna-go-fighting, Corps-loving, Who rah! Wah who! Or something like that—and ready to go into battle, storm the beach, shoot his gun, and obey the Gunny's orders. (*What an idiot*). This guy was all brainwashed into obeying orders even to storm the beach when outnumbered and fight to the death for his country. He wanted Mark and his buddy to join him and be one of the few good men they were looking for. Well, Mark and his buddy thought they were good, but not stupid. Mark looked at his buddy and both agreed that this service was not for the thinking man but the following-orders man. And this was not for them.

They then went to see the Air Force recruiter, and the deals were okay but nothing exciting. At least this recruiter was not as excited as the Marine Corp recruiter was. The Air Force recruiter said you can go to a base outside of the fighting and stay there for four years and never move. Well, that didn't sound exciting—they could do that at home. They wanted excitement, travel, to make money, and get out of their hometown. Well, they had been offered Army infantry to fight face-to-face in the jungles of Vietnam, become a trained killer for the Marines, the few, the proud, or be an Airman in the Air Force stuck on some base for four years. *Wow! Almost sounds as boring as cruising the strip in Griffith, Indiana.*

So Mark's friend said, "Let's try the Navy recruiter. We have nothing to do today, let's see what they have to offer." They walked into the office and were greeted by a Chief Petty Officer (*Whatever that meant*). He was real confident with a kind of "I don't give a shit what you think" attitude. He had his name on his desk with big anchors on it and real cool pictures and certificates on the wall. Mark thought he must be important. He never did figure out why they called him "Petty"—he seemed real important to everyone in the office. Mark's buddy said, "We are here to see what you have to offer."

The Chief said to Mark, "What do you want to do in the Navy?"

"Well, I want to be a helicopter pilot," said Mark.

The Chief, with a smug grin and looking up at the ceiling, said, "Do you have a college education?"

"No," said Mark.

"Well, son, then you cannot be a helicopter pilot."

So the Chief said, "However, let's see your test scores." Of course, he had a copy from when they came out to the high school.

He said, "Mark, you scored high in mechanics, and I can make you a jet engine mechanic. That's as close to a helicopter pilot as I can get you."

He went on, "Let me see your friend's score." After looking at it he said, "I can get the same job for your friend. As a matter of fact, I have a program that will keep you two together."

"It's called the buddy plan," he continued. "You can go to boot camp together and even be in the same company. After you complete boot camp the Navy will put you in school and teach you how to fix jet engines."

He told them that they could sail on a warship in the greatest Navy in the world, travel to foreign ports, drink beer from all parts of the world, meet exotic women, shop for things you cannot buy in the Calumet Region, and make money while doing all of this. He gave Mark and his buddy posters, bumper stickers, and pamphlets.

This was real exciting to Mark and this would help him answer the question, "Mark, what are you going to do when you grow up?" Mark was a bit nervous and even scared to leave the comfort of his home and make the decision to join the Navy. However, in this case, fear was not an option.

The U.S. Navy was the answer. Mark didn't need job experience to join the Navy. They would send him to school, and they would give him a paycheck. Mark thought this would be the answer for the next four years of his life and would provide excitement and escape from the Calumet Region and the small-town antics of Griffith, Indiana.

So the recruiter went to see Mark's parents (and his buddy's) to talk about the deal and sign papers. Of course, his parents had to sign, since Mark was under 18 years old. Most parents want to see their children grow up and get out on their own, and Mark's parents knew the Navy would be a good experience, so they agreed. The Navy recruiter made a deal to keep Mark and his best friend together through boot camp and Jet Engine Mechanics School.

The Navy called it the "buddy system" and they also signed them up on a "delayed entry program." They could sign up six months early with the condition that they graduate high school. This allowed them to take the summer off and go into the Navy in the early fall. What a deal for them, a future to sail and see the world, young and dumb teenagers. Enjoy the summer, and not have to go to school and in the fall go into the Navy.

The Navy advertised: "It's not just a job, it's an adventure."

Mark dreamed of getting out on his own, seeing the world, enjoying the adventure, and getting out of his small town. It never crossed his mind that he would have to swim. Why? Because ships float! And Mark had no intention of jumping into the water without a life vest.

Well, when the day to leave came around, Mark said goodbye to his family and got on the train for U.S. Navy Boot Camp. Welcome to Great Lakes, Illinois, and 13 weeks of training.

As you probably know, with any boot camp they cut your hair, (crew cut for the sailors), give you clothes to wear, a set of dress blues and summer dress whites, sneakers, and even a rifle to march with (of course no bullets). They tell you when to get up, how to make your bed; they feed you three times a day, tell you when to eat, when to crap, when to sleep—you don't have to think about anything!

As the Company Commander said, "I am now your mother and father," and he lets you know this quite often. He also lets you know that he will not wipe your nose or your butt. Boot camp is "a giant game of Simon Says," Your job as a good recruit is to win. Do what you are told to the letter. If you can do this for 13 weeks, then you pass. No matter what the Company Commander (Simon) says, just remember that he is right, and if you follow the leader you will stay out of trouble.

In the old-style pinball machines, the pinball is shot into the playing area. The ball doesn't have to think. The player has control of the paddles to knock it right, left, in play, out of play, and the pinball goes without thinking or having control of its destination. This was Mark's life now—he was the pinball. He did not have control of what he did, when he did it, or how he got there. The U.S. Navy had his back and planned his life and future for the next four years. All Mark had to do was follow directions—when the paddle hit him, he would move left or right. The paddle was the Company Commander, Commanding Officer, the "Chief," and any Petty Officer over him. All Mark had to do was "keep his nose clean" and perform well in school and on the job. That translated to, "Be a good pinball."

Mark did well and was a very obedient sailor. Following directions was easy for him, until the day he heard the words that scared the crap out of him. The Company Commander said, "Get your swim trunks; we're going to the pool, for a swim test."

All the familiar thoughts and fears came rushing back to him. Like getting hit in the breadbasket by a professional boxer, his knees were beginning to buckle, his stomach had butterflies, and he thought of all the failed swim tests of the past. This might be a short Navy enlistment for him, he thought. But, of course, as a good pinball, he just got whacked by the paddle and did as he was told.

When he got to the pool and smelled the chlorine, he had a vivid memory of his childhood days taking swim lessons—it all came back to him in a flash. He asked himself, "How did I get myself into this predicament? What are they going to make me do?" Would he drown this day? Would he drink chlorine water and swallow air until his stomach was full? What would he do if he could not swim to the side of the pool? Would a hand be there when he would need it? Will they kick him out of the Navy and send him home?

Mark once again, just like when he was a pre-teen, was scared shitless; he was shaking in his boots, but he knew he had to get past this. He had to try—his future depended on it. All the sailors were given swim trunks and told to change, bring their trousers back, and line up. Mark's heart was in his mouth, and he didn't know what to say or do, but as a good pinball he changed and got in line. Just putting on the swim trunks gave him a bad feeling inside.

Once all the sailors lined up, the instructor told them to climb to the platform, cross their arms over their chest (when jumping from the top deck of a ship, hitting the water with your arm out to the side will break it from the impact), and jump feet first into the 12-foot deep section. Then they said the most beautiful words: "You must jump in even if you cannot swim—we will pull you out. We don't care what stroke you use, just swim from the deep end to the shallow end and get out." *Wow, this means I can dog paddle, breaststroke—anything to get to the shallow end.* The test had no time limit, no test of the crawl stroke, and your face didn't need to go underwater.

Mark watched others in front of him struggle and cling to the side of the pool. Some were pulled out of the water because they could not swim, and others swam like a fish to the shallow end. When it was Mark's turn, he climbed the ladder to the top of the platform. It was high off the water, and the water was deep. Deep to Mark was anything deeper than what he could stand in and still get a breath of air. He closed his eyes and stepped off the platform; he did his best to get back to the surface and keep his face out of the water so he could get fresh air. He slowly dog-paddled to the shallow end of the pool, all the time swimming an arm's length from the side of the pool. All Mark needed to do was get to the shallow end of the pool without help, and he passed.

Fear had gripped Mark, but he knew he could dog-paddle, switch to the breaststroke, if needed, and make his way to the shallow end of the pool. If Mark had been given a choice, he would have run from the water and chosen not to take part in this test. However, he was in boot camp to finish and get through it.

Fear was not an option—he needed to face the fear head on and push thru it and pass this swim test because, this swim test was part of the boot camp program. Mark focused on the end result, faced the fear, and moved toward it, not away from it, and he got to the shallow end of the pool. This taught him a valuable lesson about getting past the fear and that is to focus on the end result, not the pain and fear of the moment.

"We generally change ourselves for one of two reasons: inspiration or desperation." – Jim Rohn

---

Fear is a very strong feeling that tears away any rational thinking. Fear can cause nervousness, stress, and panicked thinking that may even cause your death or the deaths of those around you. A drowning person has grabbed so tightly onto the person who is trying to save them that they have drowned the rescuer and themselves. The drowning victim never thinks to relax and let the rescuer pull them to safety.

Can fear so occupy your thoughts that you will not act, that you will not listen to reason, and will not trust others who even say, "You can do it!"? Can fear hold you back from learning, performing, and trying? Can fear consume your rational thinking? Can fear stop you from being a success even when you say you desire to succeed? Was Mark the only person who was scared of the water? No! There were others who were scared that day, and who did not pass the swim test. They had to go at night to take lessons so they could pass the test. Fear is universal, but it affects people in different situations and about different things.

Some people fear animals, snakes, spiders, and dogs. Other people fear tight spaces, traveling, public places, dark rooms, and heights.

Can fear stop people from doing things they really want to do in life? Yes, fear has stopped people throughout history from doing the things they were meant to do. Are people destined to do great things but let fear so grab them that they do not act, or are afraid of rejection, ridicule, and pain? Yes.

But how do you break the chain of events and stop the fear? Can you stop the fear by wishing for the fear to go away? The fear may be a life-saving internal alarm to warn you of danger and removing it completely would put you in a dangerous situation, without a clue that you may be in trouble.

"Our doubts are traitors and make us lose the good
we oft might win, by fearing to attempt." – William Shakespeare

---

Mark felt all these things. Mark feared the water, but instead of running away from the thing he feared, he moved reluctantly toward the thing he feared.

This is key: Mark wanted to be in the Navy and feared getting kicked out more than he feared drowning. And so Mark got to the shallow end of the pool and passed step one of the test. The instructors then said, "OK, all of you now go get your trousers and go back to the deep end of the pool." *OH! NO! NOT THE DEEP END OF THE POOL!* Mark never liked the water over his head, because he feared not being able to get air when he wanted it. So going to the deep end of the pool was the place he was most uncomfortable with.

In order to grow, or to go beyond the fear, you must leave the comfort zone and move in a zone that is uncomfortable. Once Mark decided not to run away but to be uncomfortable, he passed the first step of the swim test, and it was in this uncomfortable state that he gained a little more confidence.

"The message is clear. It is not what is happening 'out there.' It is
what is happening between your ears. It's your attitude that counts.
Get your attitude right, and chances are dramatically higher that
your economic condition will be good." – Zig Ziglar

Growth beyond fear will occur in two ways. You are either thrown into the fire for short periods of time, or you are thrown into the fire for long periods of time. Either way, you grow. Mark was thrown into the fire (the water of the pool), and he either sank or he would fight to swim.

You cannot stay in your comfort zone and expect to grow beyond your fears. As long as you stay in your comfort zone, you are comfortable. Overcoming fear requires you to go beyond the walls of your comfort zone and experience things that scare the hell out of you.

We live in a society that wants to protect us from any pain, discomfort, and make everyone equal. This will prevent us from growing. When a child rides a bike or roller skates, *they will fall down*, but it's in the getting up that they learn to ride, fall down, and get up again. It is *impossible* for an infant to walk without falling down at least once. The more we fall, the more we try not to fall down; thus we gain better balance and skills to move ahead.

Mark had his trousers and wondered what would happen next. His mind was racing, and he was still breathing hard (not from exhaustion, but from fear). The instructor said, "If the ship should sink and you jump overboard and do not have a life jacket, you can take your trousers off, tie knots in the legs and inflate them with air and float until you are rescued."

Mark thought, *is that really possible?* He also figured that he could leave his head above water and dog paddle until he figured out how to make the trousers become a float.

Mark tied knots in the pant legs and when told to jump in, he raised the pants over his head and filled them with air as he hit the water; he splashed water on the pants to keep them wet so the air would not leak out fast. Then he splashed water and air into the legs of the pants. He then put the crotch under his chest and one leg under each armpit, and he was floating. Mark had passed Step 2 of the test and was told to get out of the pool. He had passed the Navy swimming test. That was all they required. *Hooray!*

As Mark was getting dressed he sighed in relief but was still on pins and needles. Even though he was in no danger and the test was over, he could not physically calm down—his adrenaline was flowing, and his panic meter was primed.

"It is not what happens to you but how you think about what happens to you that determines how you feel and react. It is not the world outside of you that dictates your circumstances or conditions. It is the world inside you that creates the conditions of your life." – Brian Tracy

These are the lessons of life, and experiencing fear is also part of life. We cannot withhold these experiences from real Americans. Americans love the story of Mark because he adapts, improvises, and overcomes. But Mark's story is not over. It is only beginning, and if Mark knew what he would do, what he would face and experience in the future, he surely would have quit and run back to his comfort zone. Mark was slowly learning how to exist outside his comfort zone. Mark was thrown into the fire for short periods of time and was experiencing fear and success. You see, Mark was in the Navy, and the Navy goes to sea, and ships float on the water and moor up to a dock. Water will be part of Mark's life for the next four years, even if he does not have to get into the water or if he avoids the water.

CHAPTER 3

WAKE UP AND SMELL THE COFFEE

Mark was relieved to know he would not be kicked out of the Navy. He made it and now was moving forward with his future. He was going to Vietnam to fight for his country, to do his duty. He was out of the small town, and he was only looking forward now. There was no turning back. Unfortunately, Mark never got orders to ride a carrier and go to Vietnam. President Nixon decided to pull the troops out.

Mark went to Jet Engine Mechanic "A" school and graduated as an ADJ (Aviation Machinist's Mate [Jet Engine Mechanic]) Airman, and they gave him orders to Albuquerque. Now Mark knew he was a sailor and would be stationed near water, so where the heck was Albuquerque? The instructor said Albuquerque is in New Mexico. *WHAT?* Mark remembered his high school geography, and he knew New Mexico is not near the water.

So he said, "Sir, there must be a mistake. New Mexico is not near the water."

The instructor said, "Welcome to the Rio Grande Navy!" You're going to Kirtland Air Force Base in Albuquerque.

Mark said, "Sir, there must be a mistake. I am in the Navy, not the Air Force."

The instructor said, "You are a jet engine mechanic, and there are Navy planes there for you to work on. Good luck!"

Mark was depressed. No Vietnam, no riding ships, no overseas travel. What was happening to his dreams? The only bright side was that Mark did not have to worry about the water, because everything was sand and desert! Even the Rio Grande dries up to a small trickle in the summer.

---

*"If you change the way you look at things,
the things you look at change." – Dr. Wayne Dyer*

When Mark flew to Albuquerque Airport he was met by a guy named Measles. It wasn't his real name; it was a nickname he was given because when he reported for duty he contracted the measles and didn't officially report for work for a couple weeks, until he was better. So they called him Measles. Measles told Mark how lucky he was to be stationed there. The town was right outside the front gate, they had their own Navy barracks, and they could buy beer on the base.

When Mark reported for duty he met a whole new lifestyle and a whole new way to live the Navy life. Instead of the Navy owning your life and every minute, Mark basically had a 40-hour-a-week job. The rest of the time was his. At work he met a group of sailors who taught him new ways to look at work. He kept hearing about "skating" and wondered where on base he could go skating.

"Skating" was a way of looking like you are working when in reality you are doing nothing productive, just wasting time. So when someone (not the supervisors) asked what you are doing, you may say, "I am skating," or you may leave the shop and tell a friend you are going skating. Skating could be to walk to the gedunk machine and buy a Pepsi in a bottle and a bag of peanuts. The habit was to drink down the Pepsi and pour the peanuts into the bottle. You then look busy drinking a soda and spending your time trying to get the peanuts out of the bottle before the soda is gone. If you do not get all the peanuts before the soda is gone the peanuts stick to the side of the bottle and you have a hard time struggling to get the peanuts out of the bottom of the bottle.

Skating may be walking across the hangar bay, stopping by everyone and shooting the breeze for 20 minutes. It could be going to the bathroom or walking across the hangar to talk to a friend. Sometimes you would get a vehicle and go across the base and get a BLT at the Towers Snack Bar, go for a ride on the back roads of the base, or grab a tow tractor and just go for a ride across the flight line. Anything to kill time was called skating. You may grab a chair and sit outside and get a quick nap while waiting for the pilots to finish their morning meeting before flying. You see, skating is looking busy doing something or doing nothing when you really should be doing something important. It's almost like a union job, but of course we do not have unions in the Navy.

Mark spent the rest of his four years on the sidelines watching motivated sailors who used their time to move ahead in the Navy (not just getting by) and to do daring things like fly in the back seats of jet airplanes, ride in helicopters, and get medals and citations for doing exciting things. Mark did not realize that skating was just getting by and that if he wanted to move ahead in the Navy and in his life he would have to be a go-getter and a planner.

He was hanging around people who just wanted to get by in the Navy and not make it a career. He worked on the jets but never rode in one. Many of his friends were flying in the back seats of jets and riding as air crewmen on cargo and patrol planes. These were exciting things to Mark, and he did not have the opportunity to move forward. He told himself that if he ever got the chance to do exciting things he would always volunteer and would *never* miss an opportunity. Mark never thought that skating and not applying himself was hurting his chances of getting the exciting jobs. So, instead of working hard, doing more than was asked, and volunteering to do more, he chose to be a slacker, and this, in reality, is what stopped him from getting what he really wanted. But if you keep your nose clean and do your job you will be moved up anyway, and Mark gained rank to (E-4) Petty Officer 3rd Class, a low-ranking leadership position.

One day the Master Chief called Mark into his office. Mark walked in, and he was again scared because he could not think of what he did wrong. He knew he had been skating, but he didn't think anyone saw him or reported him. He also knew the Master Chief was a little weird, and Mark didn't know how to take him. The Master Chief would go to take a crap and leave the stall door wide open. Many times Mark would be looking for a place to skate and go to the bathroom and go into the stall only to find the Master Chief sitting on the shitter with his pants around his ankles staring up at him, and it would scare the living crap out of him.

Mark entered the office and took three steps. The Master Chief said, "Have a seat." "Mark, you now have become a Petty Officer, and that means you have more responsibility—you have to be a leader and soon you'll become a supervisor." He went on, "You may even have to stop hanging around with some of your old friends who have not been promoted."

He then said, "You see the plaque on the wall, there? What does it mean?" The plaque said, "Lead, follow, or get the hell out of the way." Mark had never seen that before and wasn't sure what it meant. But he was not a fan of the look on the face of the Master Chief, and he knew that the Master Chief expected an answer.

Mark took a swing at it. "It means to be the leader, if not, though, to follow the leader, and if you don't want to lead or follow, get out of the way from the other people leading and following."

The Master Chief said, "That is close, but you have to make a choice; as a Petty Officer you now are in a position of leadership. Before, when you were an airman, you followed the petty officers. Now you have to become the leader. If you don't want to become the leader, then follow the other people or get out of the way. If you do not want to lead, we can take the rank from you and give it to someone who wants to lead. You need to make a decision for your future in the Navy."

Mark thought, *What is he trying to say, and how do I comment on that?* He said, "Oh! I understand." The Master Chief continued for another 10 minutes talking about being a good sailor and doing the right things. Finally, he got done talking and told Mark to get back to work. Mark was relieved and quickly exited the office, leaving skid marks on the floor. It never was good to be called into the Master Chief's office, but it was nice to be leaving with your butt still intact.

Time went on and Mark got a little wiser, a little older, and a little less gullible. And he was sent to the fleet by way of a promised jet engine school and shore duty in California. In 1979 he was offered the opportunity to go to Miramar, California, and go to Power Plants and Related Systems School and learn how to work on the TF-30 jet engine. This was a good opportunity, because this was the engine that powered the best fighter the Navy had. It fit into the swept-wing F-14 Tomcat, and upon graduation he would go to Fighter Squadron VF-211, which was attached to the aircraft carrier USS *Constellation*. This aircraft and Naval Station Miramar became the aircraft featured in the 1986 movie *Top Gun*, with Tom Cruise, Kelly McGillis, and Val Kilmer. Mark was excited and felt that his life in the Navy was changing for the better. He worked on the aircraft, removed and replaced the jet engines, launched and recovered aircraft, and was living in California, the state known for warm weather, sunny beaches, women, fast cars, parties every night, and rock 'n' roll. But this isn't what Mark was looking for; he was looking for more excitement, a better opportunity, and moving up. Yes, working on these high-quality, professionally engineered engines that produce maximum thrust of 14,560 lbf (pounds of force), 25,100 lbf w/ afterburning—was very exciting, but there was a burning in his heart to do something great with his life. The F-14 Tomcat was a great plane to launch off the flight deck and to watch climb vertically past the clouds. But the real excitement was for the pilot. Mark thought back to the day he talked to the recruiter about being a helicopter pilot. It seemed that Mark was the spectator and not the player on the field. Mark joined for an adventure, but the more he did in the Navy the more adventure he wanted.

Soon after reporting for duty to the *Constellation* he was told he would deploy on a six-month cruise, and he was excited to be on the busiest and most dangerous piece of real estate in the world. This totally steam-driven system can rocket a 45,000-pound plane from 0 to 165 miles per hour in two seconds!

Mark thought this was cool—where could anyone go for an ocean voyage, see foreign ports, work on the most advanced aircraft in the world, see afterburners shoot a 15-foot flame out the back of an engine that launches from zero to 150+ MPH 50 feet from you and have it all paid for by the U.S. Navy and U.S. taxpayers? *WOW!* This is the excitement he was looking for

Once Mark got on board the aircraft carrier, he had to be escorted by a seasoned sailor and checked out on flight deck operations. He was told by the Petty Officer to keep his head on a swivel and watch out for your 6, or you could be killed, or even worse, get blown overboard and become shark bait. "Head on a swivel" meant to always be looking around and aware of what is happening on the flight deck. "Watch out for your 6" means to look out for your 6 o'clock position or backside, because no one cares more about your life than you.

There were lines on the flight deck that all personnel had to stay behind during recovery, because when the aircraft landed and you had crossed the line, the wing tips moving at 150 mph could take your head off. Worse than that is the fact that the Air Boss would chew your ass for crossing the line, and I think our Air Boss graduated top of the class in ass-chewing. When he chewed your ass you either became knock-kneed or bowlegged depending on where he was chewing, and when you left his office everyone knew you had your ass chewed because you could hear his voice seven bulkheads away, and because you walked funny.

Current U.S. Navy carriers have three or four steel cables stretched across the deck at 20-ft. (6.1 m) intervals that bring a plane traveling at 150 mph (240 km/h) to a complete stop in about 320 ft. (98 m). An aircraft jet engine has enough suction to lift a grown man off his feet and suck him into the engine, and if you are behind the engine it can knock a grown man off his feet and roll him down the deck and over the side. This would then be about a 90-ft. fall to the water depending on the age of the carrier. This would definitely ruin your day. At all times you need to know how close you are to a running engine's intake, and if the aircraft is turning or moving forward, you can be blown over, so you have to be especially careful where you are walking. And you have to keep in mind that the ship is in the ocean, rocking from side to side, so you have to watch your balance.

This was exciting, but for 95% of the time Mark was in the hangar bay below decks working on the aircraft, keeping them working so the pilots could fly them. It is said that the F-14 needed 34 hours of maintenance for every hour of flight time. So after a five-hour flight it will need about 60 hours of work—well you do the math. Anyway, it's a lot of work to keep these birds flying. You have to remember there are three kinds of people in the world, those who can count and those who cannot count.

Freedom is not free! One day Mark was skating and walking through the hangar bay observing all the aircraft and the different people working on the aircraft. Some people were painting the airframe, others were removing panels to access electronic components and boxes, and others were washing the aircraft, changing tires, or testing the ordnance racks. All of a sudden, Mark heard someone yelling, "What are you doing?" Mark thought someone was going to get his ass chewed, so he figured he would watch. It was a Chief Petty Officer (Chiefs run the ship, so when they talk, you better listen), and he was looking in Mark's general direction. The Chief said, "Yeah, you, get your butt over here." Mark thought, *Oh, shit, he's talking to me, now what did I do?* Mark looked around to see if he was walking in a restricted area. No, he was not, and he then glanced at his uniform, and it was in regulation, so that was not the problem either.

Mark said, "Yes, Chief." The Chief said, "What are you doing?" Now if that wasn't a loaded question. Mark thought fast, *If I say nothing, he's going to give me work to do, if I lie, he will find me out and I will be in trouble. If I answer too much he will have more questions.* So Mark told the truth and said, "I am going to supply." The Chief said, "You look like you are in the zoo, strolling along looking at the monkeys. Do you need something to do?"

Mark said, "No, Chief." The Chief said, "Do you have a clipboard?" Mark said, "No" (not wanting to provide too much information). "OK," the Chief said, "you get yourself a clipboard so you look busy and pick up your pace like you are going somewhere, and if you keep gawking at the aircraft and walk like you have nothing to do, someone will find work for you. You are a 2nd class Petty Officer, so look busy even if you are not."

Mark said, "Yes, Chief," and continued to walk away at a very brisk pace. Mark thought, *That was some good information, the Chief taught me a new way to look busy.* When he got back to the shop he got a clipboard and put some papers on it, and from then on when he walked in the hangar bay, he walked fast and kept the clipboard with him wherever he went, even when he went to lunch.

Mark was now the busiest looking person in the Navy. He would take two steps at a time when going up the stairs and he slid down the railings on the way down. Looking busy and in a hurry became his goal. When he was in a meeting, out came the clipboard or wheel book (small note pad that fits into your pocket). He would write a shopping list, doodle, or make a list of things to do, but everyone saw him as someone who pays attention and takes a lot of notes. Perception is everything.

Then the day came where they needed a troubleshooter from the power plant division to work on the flight deck. There were other jet engine mechanics more qualified than Mark to work on the flight deck, but they were scared to work up on the flight deck. Again, Mark saw this as an opportunity to do something more exciting, but why were these guys turning it down? Was there something Mark was not seeing? Did they know something about this job that Mark did not?

Then the boss came to Mark and said, "Would you like to work on the flight deck?"

Mark said, "What do I have to do?"

The boss said, "You would be a "troubleshooter"—you would have to be on the deck whenever our aircraft are launched and recovered from a mission. It will be for daytime flights and night flights. You will have to evaluate the aircraft's airframe and power plants for correct operation prior to launch. You will have the authority to stop the launch of the aircraft if you see anything that is not right. You will also be responsible for giving thumbs up, saying the aircraft is ready for flight and the pilot will be putting his trust in you." See the following video for more information:

http://www.youtube.com/watch?v=vro1wKaOu-Q

Mark knew this was another opportunity to move up. He would have more responsibility, he would be with the pilots, and he would be on the flight deck, where all the action is. So he jumped on the opportunity and told the boss he would do it.

For the rest of the cruise Mark would be working on the flight deck; he would be standing 10 feet from the wing tip and within 20 feet of the afterburner when the F-14 launched from the steam- powered catapult. To Mark, this was sooo cool. When the afterburner turned on, it had five stages and the heat was so intense that it felt like the plastic goggles were melting on his face. Mark had to shield his face with his arm as he was holding the thumbs up signal that it was good to launch. There was always something new going on up on the flight deck. Every mission was different, and the pilots changed. The aircraft was parked in different positions and the weather was different on the deck. This is what Mark wanted. His life had more meaning and he felt important because he was the last person to look at the aircraft before it left the deck and he had to give either the thumbs up or thumbs down and stop the flight. While on the cruise, Iran decided to take some Americans hostage for some reason that Mark didn't understand. But it didn't matter if he understood or not. The carrier USS *Constellation* was told that it needed to change its plans and go directly to the Indian Ocean to stand by if needed to attack Iran or whatever mission was assigned. Mark thought he might see some action, but he knew that some ports of call were cancelled and they would have to stay in the Indian Ocean, making circles, until another carrier came to relieve them. Well, it so happened that they stayed at sea without a port of call for 110 days. This was a long time at sea.

One day while Mark and his fellow troubleshooters were on deck waiting for the launch to begin they were talking about why they were at sea. Mark asked, "Why are we here?" Of course, the answer was, the Navy told them to be there.

Mark said, "Be more specific."

One guy said, "Because I was tired of my hometown, and I wanted to see the world." Another said, "If I stayed at home, I would probably be in jail—I had to get away."

Another said, "I got kicked out of the house, and the Navy said they will pay me for four years; maybe it's for the security."

Mark said, "But why are we here in the Indian Ocean?"

One troubleshooter said, "We are here because we volunteered to be in the Navy, which protects the seas so pirates and other countries' navies will not attack the United States and in order to keep the shipping lanes open, just like we were taught in school."

The other troubleshooter said, "Yeah! We are here so my family at home will feel safe and can have a good job, own property or a business in a land that is free."

Mark said, "So it is about freedom, we are doing our time here so others will be free at home, and when we return, there will be another carrier doing this so we will be free in the United States."

All us troubleshooters had a moment of insight, and reflection, and suddenly their job took on more meaning for them—it became a bigger cause than just making money or taking orders.

We had a mission of giving Americans security and freedom at home. It didn't make the 110 days easier, but Mark didn't seem to complain as much from that day forward. Well, as it turned out, they were relieved by another carrier and were sent into port, which was needed badly for the crew, who needed to blow off steam. It was now 1981, and the carrier headed for Singapore. When they got there many sailors were looking for women, whisky, beer, and good food, but not in that order. Of course, when you mix alcohol, women, sailors, and transvestites on hotel street, in Singapore after 110 days at sea you are looking for trouble. And of course there was fighting that first night between sailors and local people and we had an international incident that made the carrier leave port early. However, Mark was able to get a bus tour, a little shopping, and a few beers before he left. Even though the port of call was cut short, the whole crew had time to relax after the long time at sea. Singapore was noted as one of the cleanest port on all of his Westpac.

Mark enjoyed the flight deck, the foreign ports, and the camaraderie of some of the crazy sailors he met during the cruise. Unfortunately, the day came to leave the aircraft carrier and go back to Miramar and work in the hangar on the F-14 aircraft. Bummer for Mark! He still stayed a troubleshooter, but the fast- paced excitement of the flight deck was over.

Well, another day came that offered change, excitement, and another opportunity. The Navy was moving into a new generation. They turned over their reciprocating engine aircraft to the Naval Reserves and had moved into exclusively using the jet engine aircraft. A reciprocating engine has pistons and propellers. So how did this affect Mark? The Navy took the reciprocating engine mechanics and made them jet engine mechanics, thus overloading the jet engine mechanic field. So when it became time to reenlist, he was given the choice to drop down one rank and stay in, get out of the Navy, or to retest for another job in the Navy. Mark knew that dropping a rank would not only be harder on his job and that it would take time to make the rank back but it would also be a loss in pay, and that was not acceptable. So he decided to take the Armed Services Vocational Aptitude Battery (ASVAB) test. Well, since his initial enlistment he had gained skills and knowledge, and much to his surprise he scored high enough for any electronic field. Since he was in aviation already, he decided to become an aviation electronics technician.

The Navy made him another deal, and since he decided to not pass up an opportunity, he went for it. They said they would send him to school and if he passed the school he would reenlist for six years so that the Navy can get their invested time and money back. If he failed at school, he would stay a jet engine mechanic, lose a rank, and return to the fleet and finish his enlistment. This was an opportunity that he knew he had to grab. If he did not pass, then he would lose.

He was sent to school for electronics in Millington, Tennessee. This proved to be a significant milestone and turning point in Mark's life. When he got to school they sent him and all the other electronics students to a classroom where they were told they had to take a math test. Again Mark was worried that this could this be a deal breaker. Mark struggled in high school to get a C in geometry and passed algebra with C's and D's. He never took trigonometry, physics, or calculus. They were told the test had basic math, geometry, algebra, trigonometry, and calculus. The instructor said, "Do your best." Mark thought, *Holy shit—just when I think things are starting to get better, they really get worse.* Just as Mark thought, he scored very badly, as did many of the other students taking the test.

The instructor called off all the names of those who scored poorly and told them to go to the next room where the instructor there said, "The Navy doesn't throw people out of a program for poor math. He went on, "We will fix you, and all of you that scored poorly will be lucky enough to go to a two-week math class. In the two-week course we will take you from addition and subtraction through geometry, algebra, trigonometry, and calculus. It's the Navy's math crash course."

Mark's mouth dropped wide open—they might as well have told him, "We are going to teach you to fly and throw you off the building."

Who were they kidding? Mark couldn't get higher than a C in algebra and that was a full semester, over four months. Now they were going to teach him trig and calculus on top of the algebra? And the instructor was not kidding—he was serious about this two-week crash course. *Could it be possible to bring people up to speed in just two weeks?*

In life, things don't move until they are pushed; it's a law of physics (an object at rest tends to stay at rest, an object in motion tends to stay in motion until another force changes it), and the Navy was pushing all of the poor math students. This would be a challenge for Mark and the rest of the sailors. The instructor said to go home and be back in the morning for day one of accelerated math.

All the students had that look on their face. "What look?" you may ask? The look that Mark knew all too well—the "what the hell did I get myself into?" look, the "I'm scared I will fail" look, and the "how the hell do I get out of here?" look. Even though he nervous about the math class he knew that times like this when he was challenged that there was a breakthrough in his life. So, Mark knew that he would be there in the morning and give it his best try, because he knew that if he didn't go down this road, then he would go back to the fleet as a jet engine mechanic with less money and no better future to look forward to.

Mark also believed that God will put you to a test in life, and he believed that if he really wanted to learn this material, he must do his part and show up and try hard, and if it was God's will, then God will help Mark in the areas that he needed help in. Anytime you have a dream, especially a big dream, God must be part of it; you do not have all the skills, all the answers, or all the endurance on your own. You need divine help, and Mark prayed and went to church often.

When Mark sat down in the classroom on day one the instructor came in and introduced himself—he said he was a retired Chief and that he loved math. He told everyone that you can and will learn more about math in two weeks than you have learned your whole life, because all your life you have been taught math in the wrong way.

He said, "You were taught to add and subtract from right to left with no clue what the answer may be until you get to the last number on the left. You need to add and subtract from left to right and immediately you know how big of a number the answer will be."

He then asked everyone in class; when they see a license plate on a car do they see patterns? When they buy food do they compare price, quantity, or package size? When they see numbers do they see patterns to the numbers, even or odd numbers, prime numbers, or numbers in a sequence? Is it easy for you to remember numbers? If so, then you have an active left side of the brain for calculations, logical abilities and math functions. He then said, this class will be easier for you than those who are right brain creative thinkers.

This instructor clearly loved math and teaching. He not only taught numbers and formulas but he told the students what the formula was for computing. He said one algebraic formula was used in building bridges to compute the strength and load, and another formula was used in weigh scales for weighing trucks. By doing this he allowed the student to see the purpose of learning the formulas and how they are used in real life.

In high school the answer to the formulas was the only thing of importance, not its use in life. This new thinking about math made every formula valuable. When he got into trigonometry he showed how the formulas were used in electronic circuits, in transistors, MOSFETs, JFETs, and integrated circuits, and it made every formula a valuable set of A's, B's, and C's, and the X and Y that had no meaning in high school now had a meaning in the formula. He told the students about using math to buy cheese and underwear in the store and how to determine the value of products, which gave the formulas life and meaning to each student. Math was interesting, because each formula had a story told by this enthusiastic retired Chief.

He was the most inspiring instructor Mark had come across. In fact, one day he said, "How many of you sailors would like to know the secret to becoming a Chief or even make the next highest rank?" Mark and many other students raised their hands.

He said, "OK, there is enough interest. Those of you who raised your hand, stay after class and I will tell you how to do it."

Mark thought, *Wow another opportunity for advancement. I will definitely be there!*

Well, after class those that were not interested got up and left and the students who stayed made up about half the class. The first thing the instructor said was to look around the class and see how many of you stayed and how some who raised their hands left.

"This is normal in life," he said. "There are people who do not look for advice, or secrets to get ahead, and there are even those who say they want to and raise their hand but when it comes down to it they get up and leave. You are the student who will not only get this valuable information, but I venture to say that all of you will pass this electronics course because you are motivated enough to stay here on your own time to listen to information that will help you get ahead in life."

He went on, "And if you apply what I say, you will be a Chief in the U.S. Navy."

Mark thought how lucky he was to be in this class—God truly had a good purpose for Mark scoring poorly on the math test. God can turn a bad situation into a great opportunity.

The Chief said, "Everything that you do from this day forward will be focused on making Chief. It must be deliberate and planned and it must be better than your peers. When you walk up the stairs and everyone takes one stair at a time, you take two. You come to work five minutes ahead of everyone and go home five minutes after the last person. You do a minimum of one correspondence course every quarter—this shows your supervisors constant improvement in the area of your education.

"Start off taking a correspondence course with only one page of questions and then two pages of questions, this way you can knock them out fast and get better at taking correspondence courses. Get all of your Navy classes converted to college credits. You will not have to take a physical education course because boot camp will give you college credits for physical education, you will not need some math classes, because this electronics course will wipe them out. Once you convert your Navy education to college equivalent credits, then take college classes and get your associate's degree and then your bachelor's degree. The four-year degree will set you above most sailors and show motivation, and this will help you to make Chief.

"Get any ribbons (like sharpshooter for pistol and rifle), letters of appreciation, and letters from any civilian organization (Boy Scouts, church groups, school help) and volunteer for extra work and extra projects. Everything you do from now on must set you above your peers and above all other sailors, and then at the selection board your package will stand out.

"Your uniform needs to be ironed, even your work clothes, and you should never get told to get a haircut, to polish your boots, or to put on clean clothes. Never be late for any meetings, or for work, and relieve the watch early and do not complain if you are relieved late. You must stand out above everyone else. Get any awards, or medals like air warfare pins, surface warfare pins, damage control pqs (personal qualification standards) signed off. Make your service record bigger and thicker than other sailors' records.

"All these things will be hard to do at first, but once they become a habit and part of the way you do business, it will become easy. Professionalism is something you learn and practice—it is not something you're born with. Being a professional sailor and a career sailor is not for everyone, and some of you will leave here today thinking I am crazy, but some of you will do as I say and you will become a Chief in the United States Navy. A Chief in the U.S. Navy is the only congressionally appointed enlisted rank in all of the four services. Only Congress can take it away from you once you are appointed to the rank of Chief in the U.S. Navy. It is a privilege and an honor that is not easy to get."

He said, finally, "In a nutshell, you must be better than other sailors in all aspects of your job and military life."

Mark left that day feeling that the retired Chief was talking directly to him and that now he held the secret to moving ahead in the Navy.

This was the opportunity Mark was looking for—and to think that he had to score poorly on a math test to be put into a class with an instructor who not only had great math knowledge but was willing to give his time to share secrets of excelling in the military.

CHAPTER 4

CREATING VISION

While he was in electronics school he applied what he learned from the Chief and excelled in the class, graduating in the top 95%. Because of his high scores he was offered a chance to ride in helicopters. He was offered a chance to try out for helicopter aircrewman. He had wanted to be a helicopter pilot since he was 15 years old, and now he had a chance to get even closer. This may be his only chance, and he would have to take it. Mark was thrilled to be offered an exciting set of orders, but—he would have to pass an aircrew physical and swim test to get this opportunity. *WOW!* Get orders as an aircrewman and fly in helicopters and airplanes and jets. This is it; this is Mark's chance to be somebody in the Navy. He would have a good set of orders, exercise, and be in top physical shape. "It's not just a job, it's an adventure." Mark was excited, but what should he do? It was obvious; the chance may never come again. Mark was scared, but he knew he had to try. This was another opportunity that came his way, and he wouldn't pass it up. Mark asked the big question, "What is in the swim test?"

He was told: "The aircrewman class II swim test consists of a deep-water jump from a platform, 100-yard swim demonstrating 25 yards each of the crawl stroke, breaststroke, sidestroke, and elementary backstroke. Immediately after the completion of the swim, without leaving the water, students will float for five minutes."

Mark was scared, but he broke the test down and thought he could go 25 feet doing the crawl without taking a breath. Then he could, he thought, transition to a stroke where his face is out of the water. As long as his face was out of the water and he could breathe, he felt sure he could pass. He had nothing to lose. Mark was now 24 years old. He was still afraid of the water, but he could do a little backstroke, and a sidestroke, because he could keep his head above water, and he knew the basic idea of the crawl stroke and of course the dog paddle. Mark wanted more excitement and to do something great with his life and for the Navy. Fear in this case was not an option. He needed to push himself and take the test in spite of his fears.

The day came that he went to the pool for the swim test, and when he walked into the pool from the shower area, the strong smell of chlorine brought back all the past fears. He felt like he was hit with a 50-pound sack of crap. Mark was thinking of the time when he was 10 years old and taking swim lessons. He felt the fear of the water, he was nervous, felt tightness in his chest, and his heart was pounding. Mark had to interrupt his remembering, though, and he needed to focus his attention on removing the fear and acting confidently—he needed to get mentally ready for the swimming test.

As much as he tried to get control of his thoughts, the little voice in his head said: *What are you doing here? Who do you think you are, applying for this when you know you can't swim for crap? Are you just wasting the instructor's time?* When he was in line with the other people there, he knew they would pass, but this test was for him still a challenge. However, Mark was older and wiser now, and he pushed himself onward.

Well, Mark was not sure of himself at all and was not demonstrating confidence with the strokes, and the swim instructor kept stopping him and telling him his style was not right.

"Glide longer, kick harder—you have poor form," the instructor said, and at the end of the test Mark was told that he failed to complete the swim test as required.

He was told he could not do the crawl and that his form for the sidestroke and breaststroke was bad, and he didn't glide and rest right.

He was told to practice more and retest at a later date. Mark was upset and knew he missed his chance to ride in helicopters. He would now have to accept the orders to the fleet and once in the fleet it would be three years before he would get a chance for new orders.

Yes, Mark now felt like the bag of crap he was hit with broke open on him, he was tired, scared, relieved to be out of the pool, embarrassed, and disappointed. Mark again was a failure in the water; being a part of the aircrew was now out of the picture. Mark would go back now to riding a ship and watching others have fun. He would never be a strong swimmer, and he will always have a life jacket as his swim buddy. Fear of the water held him back again.

Mark made a big mistake, and that was doing what he had always done. If you keep on doing what you are doing you will keep on getting what you are getting. He did nothing to prepare for this test. He did not have a plan to get ready for the swim test, he did not practice the swimming strokes, he figured with time he would somehow know how to swim. But how many times do we see people that want to change, they say they will and have all the good intentions, but do not have a plan or the resolve to do it?

Anytime you want to change what you are doing you must decide to do it, make a plan, and never quit till you achieve it, especially if you have to overcome fear or criticism. Since Mark did not pass the swim test, guess where the Navy was going to send him. You got it. Back to the fleet! However, they needed to give him a specialty, so they chose Doppler radar school so he could fill an empty billet (position) in the electronics division.

While he was at radar school there was a uniform inspection. This is normal practice for keeping the sailors looking good. Of course, it was on a Monday morning, first thing. Now during the weekend Mark was not even thinking about Monday morning; in fact, work was the farthest thing from his mind. This was to prove to be a big mistake.

Well, Monday morning came and he grabbed his pressed uniform, got dressed, and went to the inspection, but when he was standing in line he noticed he forgot one little detail. He forgot to shine his shoes, and compared to the other sailors his shoes looked like crap. You know the saying; He doesn't know shit from Shinola. (*Shinola* is a brand of wax *shoe polish* that was available in the early- to mid-twentieth century.) Well, it looked like he polished his shoes with a rock. Mark knew he was in trouble, but it was too late to do anything. He took the toe of his left shoe and wiped it on the back of his right calf and did the same with his right foot but they still looked like crap, no shine and dirt around the soles. Maybe the inspector will miss them, Mark thought. Well, to make a long story longer, Mark was hit on the inspection for unshined shoes, and he had to go see the Master Chief in his office before the end of the day.

It was always something; Mark's habits were getting him into trouble. So at lunch time Mark went to see the Master Chief. He walked into the office and said, "Master Chief, I failed the inspection and was told to come and see you."

The Master Chief said, "Why did you fail?"

Mark thought, if I say I did not shine my shoes, then this may be a 20-minute ass-chewing about preparedness, responsibility, and setting a good example—so Mark said, "My shined shoes were at home."

The Master Chief looked at him and said, "You need to have inspection shoes and working shoes, and everyone makes a mistake. So next time wear your inspection shoes to the inspection and not your working shoes."

This was another good piece of information for Mark to digest. You have inspection clothes and shoes, and you have working clothes and shoes. This time he didn't get an ass-chewing, just a simple mistake.

Then the Master Chief said "Okay, find your name on this list and sign your name."

Oh no! Mark did not have a pen. Mark said, "Ahh, Master Chief do you have a pen I could borrow?"

The Master Chief said, "What? You are a second class petty officer and you do not have a pen on you?"

The Master Chief, reaching for his pen, said, "Here is a pen, keep this, and don't let me ever see you without a pen. You must be an example to the lower ranks and you must be prepared for work. How can you take notes if you do not have a pen?"

"Yes, Master Chief," Mark said. He signed the paper and got out of his office as fast as he could before the Master Chief could find something else wrong.

New information—carry a pen and have inspection shoes and working shoes. To make a long story longer, Mark graduated Doppler radar school and was on his way to another aircraft carrier, the USS *Ranger* in North Island, San Diego, California. Here Mark was watching others do exciting things and living their dreams and most of all "living Mark's dreams." So again Mark was on an aircraft carrier, but he was working in the avionics branch and in the Comm/Nav Div. (Communications and Navigation division). It was an important job to keep the UHF, VHF, and HF radios, Tacan, IFF (Identification Friend or Foe), and Radar working for the carrier's aircraft. It was a nice change to sit in an air-conditioned space on the ship. You had clean clothes and a clean work space, unlike the flight deck with its grease, fuels, exhaust, loud engines, and dangerous conditions. Mark felt like this was a good change and he enjoyed his time on the cruise, but something was still missing.

Time went on, and Mark gained maturity and the drive to do something great for his country. It was about this time that the John Anthony Walker case broke open, a case of espionage. Walker was caught selling codes for U.S. radio transmissions and gave classified documents to the Russians. Mark's patriotism and love for his country found this appalling. He couldn't understand how that man could do what he did, sell out his country, and put fellow sailors' lives in jeopardy. Most of all, he wondered how good patriots and loyal sailors could turn down this job, handling classified material and allow this America-hating person an opportunity to get his hands on this material and turn it over for money—and put the lives of many American sailors at risk.

Mark vowed to take a job handling classified material to do his duty and stop dirt bags from getting their hands on classified material and holding positions like this. If every patriotic sailor stood up to the plate and took high-risk jobs it would reduce the chance for America-hating sailors to get an opportunity to sell out America. Mark decided to move out of the Communication/Navigation (Comm/Nav) division and work in the Crypto office behind locked doors. He would soon be the supervisor of this office and would work with the daily codes used to encrypt radios. So Mark went to Crypto school, got a secret clearance, and then went to school to repair the electronic boxes. This meant more responsibility, more excitement, more time to complete correspondence courses and to work on his Aviation Warfare Wings. He was working the plan given to him by the retired Chief in math school. He was a supervisor, he guarded classified material, and he enjoyed the responsibility.

About a year later they had the annual physical training test for the sailors, and Mark's whole division had to show up in physical training gear. During the test he watched his Senior Chief almost die in the annual 1.5-mile run and Navy physical training test. The test consisted of pull-ups, sit-ups, push-ups, 1.5-mile run, and toe touch. They were done at 9:00 a.m., and the senior chief was white as a ghost. He was 37 years old and would retire from the Navy in another year. The Senior Chief went home for the rest of the day and lay on the couch.

Mark knew this was a very easy test and that if he continued on this career path, he would be like the Senior Chief at retirement. *NO WAY!* Mark again took a stand to never allow himself to get out of shape like the Senior Chief. He didn't want to be like that, so Mark decided to get in shape and stay in shape. Mark started his own exercise program partly from a book called *Get Tough* and partly from his own ideas. He would exercise five days a week and he would do something every day. He would mix up running, biking, and swimming. He used the presidential physical fitness program to track his progress, and he received a patch and certificate as an incentive for completing the program's standards. He rode his 10-speed bike to work and after work went to the gym. He walked at lunch and parked his car on the far side of the parking lot, and he did what he could to stay in shape. He knew he needed a better workout and something that he could do on his lunch hour. The problem was that he only had an hour to change clothes, exercise, shower, and get back to work. He decided to go to the pool for a change so he could exercise different muscle groups. He would also save time changing and showering.

The pool was run by the U.S. Navy divers. They had two missions: one was to operate and be safety swimmers for the Dilbert Dunker, and the second was recruiting divers for the Navy. What is a Dilbert Dunker? It's a device for training pilots on how to correctly escape a submerged plane. It was invented by Wilfred Kaneb, a nautical engineer, during World War II. The device was featured in the 1982 film, *An Officer and a Gentleman*, starring Richard Gere and Debra Winger.

The dunker, like in the movie, is used to simulate your aircraft crashing into the water and turning upside down. The pilot has to unbuckle his seat belt from the aircraft and swim to the surface. The divers are there to help if they're needed.

Mark figured he could swim near the side of the pool an arm's length from the side and work different muscle groups, shower, and get back to work in an hour. He didn't care about the dunker or the divers—he only wanted to stay in shape. Mark swam the breaststroke and sidestroke, and started off with the goal of doing five laps and slowly increasing it. With these strokes he could keep his head out of the water, and he felt safe near the side of the pool.

The divers then talked with Mark and began to recruit him. They asked him if he ever thought of being a diver. They told him of the exciting life of a diver, physical training every day as part of your job, repairing ships, retrieving lost items that fall into the water, and going after planes that crash into the ocean.

This is not what Mark wanted, but it was interesting to think of the excitement and doing something great for America and to *stay in shape* at the same time. Then the divers said that to get in the program you had to take a swim test and you could only do the sidestroke and breaststroke (these were called "resting strokes"). Why? Because these are the two strokes that you can do with scuba tanks on, and they allow you to glide with a rest for long-distance swimming.

This sounded too good to be true! Mark was excited. But little did he know that it takes hard work, a lot of swimming in the water, and a swim test. The dreaded swim test! Mark thought it was another dream out of reach for him. So he didn't give it much thought.

As luck had it, and God's plan, there was a bomb threat called into the electronics building where Mark worked, and the U.S. Navy Explosive Ordnance Disposal (EOD) responded. These guys were buffed—they were in shape—and they had a cool uniform that separated them from the Navy Blue sailor outfit. But who were these guys? Where did they come from, and how come he never heard of them?

Mark decided to find out what they did. He didn't even know the Navy had a bomb squad. Now Mark kept to himself and was a bit shy, but his fear of talking to a group of special operations guys was overcome by his curiosity to find out what these guys did. So he walked up and asked them what they did and why they were there. They said we are the bomb squad and we are standing by. Mark asked, "Shouldn't you be in the building looking for the bomb?"

One of them said to him, "No way! If we go in there, every box, suitcase, and package is suspect. If the people who work there look, they will be able to rule out the suitcases, boxes, and packages that are theirs, and a suspicious package is the only package we will work on."

That made a lot of sense to Mark. So they just stood by, that sounded cool.

They told Mark that being an EOD diver was better then being a Navy diver, because the Navy divers dive in the *mud* and the crap dumped overboard from the ships. They told Mark that EOD gets to do demolition on the land and underwater, and that they have classified publications and must get a security clearance to get in. They also had physical training two hours a day and drank beer.

Wow! Handling classified material (a plus), physical training two hours a day to stay in shape (plus #2), demolition (plus #3), travel overseas, and dive the oceans of the world (*Wow! But wait, that means water, fear, failure*). The big decision, stay with the electronics and look like the Senior Chief or find a different job, a more exciting job, and stay in shape at the same time. Mark walked away excited, but scared. He was hopeful, but had the taste of failure in his mouth. Could he ever be as successful and in good shape as these guys? The dream seemed so far away.

Mark was dreaming again. He had hopes of a better job, and he really wanted to do something great, but the water was his greatest fear. Does he give up on a dream and let fear rule, or should he try again with the possibility of failure? Mark was *not* a quitter, and he really did want to win. Mark felt the pulling at his heart to do more with his life, and it seemed that every time he saw a good opportunity and a good job, it had to do with the water and swimming or diving.

After talking with the Navy divers and EOD, he knew two things clearly: (1) If he ever wanted another chance to do something meaningful, he must pass the physical training test, and (2) if he did not want to lose his health like his Senior Chief did, he would have to set up a physical training program for himself. So Mark did anything he could do in order to exercise during the day. He rode his bike to and from work a couple of days a week. He ran after work at the base gym, he left his car in the parking lot and walked when possible. He even took a couple of lunch hours and hit the base pool and swam at lunch for the next nine months.

Fortunately, Mark was up for reenlistment in a year, so he talked to the career counselor. Mark was 29 years old, and the career counselor said the cutoff age for the divers, EOD (Explosive Ordnance Disposal), and SEAL (Sea Air Land) programs was 30 years old. So Mark knew he would have to work fast. He had only one year left before he would not be eligible for these programs. He was now under pressure and had to make a decision to let the opportunity slip by or to go for it. But which program?

"I used to say, 'I sure hope things will change.' Then I learned that the only way things are going to change for me is when I change." – Jim Rohn

---

Mark sat down and asked himself if he liked the way he was living, the job he was doing, and the people he was associating with. So he said to himself, "If I do not like the direction of my life, then I must—I *must*—change the direction." This was a tough question to ask and to answer.

"You cannot change your destination overnight, but you can change your direction overnight." – Jim Rohn

---

Mark thought back to:

- the Master Chief nine years earlier who challenged him to lead, follow, or get out of the way
- to the Chief on the Hangar Bay who wanted him to pick up his pace and look busy
- to the retired Chief who taught him how to be in the top 5% and how to move up in rank

Then he thought of the EOD guys. They looked professional, acted cocky—they were in top physical shape and were happy diving and responding to bomb calls.

Mark knew that if things in his life were going to change, then *he* had to change first. That day he took his clipboard out and started a plan that would lead him for the next nine months.

1. Get educated—buy books on physical fitness and swimming.
2. Talk to people who have done what you want to do—the EOD guys.
3. Set a nine-month plan to be in shape to take the physical entrance test.
4. Request in writing to leave electronics and go to EOD School.
5. Complete the Navy Diver correspondence course to see if that job interested him, and then take a scuba diving class. Why waste the Navy's time and money if it's not for him?

Mark was fortunate to have had leaders who gave him good advice. When the student is ready, the teachers will appear, and Mark did listen and was ready and waiting for an opportunity to appear.

Whatever your situation, there is a strategy that will make you a winner. Mark's strategy was perseverance, never quitting, and working hard to get in shape. So, for the next nine months Mark hit the gym and followed the book *Get Tough*, which was written by an ex-Navy SEAL.

While at the gym he met many other sailors working out and getting into shape. He was talking with a man named Matt and he said he was also getting in shape to go to the SEALs. So Matt and Mark met at the gym twice a week and motivated each other, exercised, and talked and dreamed about their futures.

Mark requested the EOD physical training test and asked for an age waiver to go to EOD School because he would be beyond the age of 30 after he finished the course. Two months later Mark's chance came and *the waiver was approved*.

Mark knew that only two swim strokes were allowed in the Navy diver, EOD, and SEAL swim tests. Those were the breaststroke and the sidestroke, both of which allowed Mark to keep his head out of the water. At the end of the nine months of his plan, Mark was swimming a mile three times a week and was very good with the breaststroke, but he still *could not swim the crawl*. Would anyone ever find out that he was afraid to swim with his face in the water? Would anyone know the fear he felt when he smelled chlorine? Would anyone know he was scared to go underwater?

Mark wrestled with the fact that he was scared but at the same time wanted to do something more exciting with his life—travel around the world, do underwater demolition, blow things up, and protect classified material. He wanted the EOD job. The Navy EOD job requires you to be a diver, but how can you get a mine or torpedo out of the water unless you dive in the water and find it and tie a rope to it? So if he has to go to EOD School he will have to go to Navy Dive School first and pass. Mark decided to take a scuba diving class and see if he could pass that. If not, then there is no need to waste the Navy's time.

"The great breakthrough in your life comes when you realize that you can learn anything you need to learn to accomplish any goal that you set for yourself. This means there are no limits on what you can be, have, or do." – Brian Tracy

Mark was scared someone would find him out, and he was scared of failing again. Mark was no different than any other person who is scared to do something—scared to get out of his or her comfort zone and take a risk. Fear needed to take a back seat to his dreams. He decided that fear was not an option if he was to become a Navy Diver. He decided to push himself to do what he feared.

The voices in his head said he could not swim well, and to be a Navy diver required someone who is a strong swimmer. Who was he kidding? Yet his heart was pulling him to move forward and to be more than an average sailor. He knew he was destined to do something great, and he had to follow his dream, leave his comfort zone, and go beyond the voices in his head that said he could not do this. He had to go beyond the smell of chlorine, the shaking when he was cold and scared, and he had to go beyond the voices of his friends who said he was crazy giving up a good career in electronics to dive in the water, work hard running, and doing pull-ups and push-ups.

Mark took the scuba diving class, and because he had air with him, he could see everything clearly with his mask, and he did not have to swim any specific stroke, he was able to feel moderately comfortable in the water. And he passed the scuba class. Now he felt he might have a good chance of passing the Navy diver portion of EOD School.

Mark saw the bigger picture and knew he would provide a greater service to his country and the U.S. Navy by being an Explosive Ordnance Disposal Technician and Navy diver. The prerequisite to be an Navy Explosive Ordnance Disposal Technician requires you to pass Navy Dive School. That makes sense, because if you have to get a mine or torpedo out of the water to dispose of it, you must at some point get in the water. Now aspiring Army, Marine, and Air Force EOD technicians do not have to go to Navy Dive School. When Army, Marine, and Air Force EOD technicians find ordnance in the water, they call the Navy for help. The pull at his heart to become Navy EOD was greater than the potential disappointment of trying and failing. Mark thought it would be better to try and to fail than to never try at all. This was his last chance for the excitement of a lifetime. He submitted the paperwork requesting a school start date for the EOD School, and he didn't reconsider his decision.

To try out for the EOD program, you had to score 110 points on the ASVAB test (Armed Services Vocational Aptitude Battery) in WK and AR (word knowledge and arithmetic). That score meant one was in the upper 5% of the Navy. Mark was fortunate—he had scored 134 points when he'd taken the test earlier to get in the electronics field, and was good to go. All he was deficient in was the physical training/swim test.

Then the day came that Mark was not ready for. The day that all people must face, the day when they want to do something out of the normal, to do something great with their life, (something that only the top 5% of sailors get a chance to try out for). Then someone asks the question you are not ready for…

The Senior Chief (his boss) called Mark into his office. *What was this all about?* Mark thought. He wondered what he did wrong, because the tone of voice and the urgency was not normal. He knew he did something wrong. *What did I forget to do, or what did I do that I shouldn't have? Okay, tuck your shirt in so you look good for the butt-chewing.*

He had been called into the office before, so he grabbed a clipboard, got a pen, made sure his uniform looked good—why? Because he was a pinball and knew the drill!

But when he went in the office, the Senior Chief had that no-nonsense look on his face and Mark knew the crap was going to hit the fan; this was not his good face, so he knew it wasn't an award ceremony. Mark snapped to attention.

"You wanted to see me, Senior Chief," he said.

"Come in, close the door, and sit down," the Senior Chief said. Mark closed the door and sat down. *Oh! The way he said that does not sound good.*

The Senior Chief said, "Mark, what's wrong? You can tell me, is your marriage bad, do you have a death wish? You don't have to be a diver. You don't have to do this, you have a comfortable job in the electronics field, you are good at what you do. Tell me what is wrong—I can help."

Mark's mouth dropped open and he said, "What do you mean, Senior Chief?"

The Senior Chief continued, "What have you done wrong? Are you having an affair, getting a divorce, do you need to leave town, do you need to see a psychologist? Do you have some kind of a death wish? I am here to help you, you can trust me. What's wrong?"

Mark was relieved that he didn't do anything wrong—the Senior Chief just thinks he is crazy, that's all.

Mark told the Senior Chief everything was fine, but the Senior Chief didn't believe him. He told the Senior Chief that he wanted excitement in his career, and that the career counselor talked to him about his future enlistment options. Mark wanted a move up; he had been to AVIC-7 electronics school (advanced electronics) and the Navy had nothing more to offer, but the diver program, the SEALS and EOD, offered excitement, dive pay, demolition pay, physical training, great health coverage, travel, exciting jobs, medals, awards, and women— well, Mark wasn't looking for women since he was married and happy.

Mark told the Senior Chief he had his mind set on passing the physical training and swim test and going to Dive School. The Senior Chief said, "You are throwing away a good career and future in electronics to work with a bunch of egomaniacs, women-chasing, beer-drinking, yahoos."

The Senior Chief thought Mark was crazy, but he wasn't willing to say it. He told Mark that his door was always open if he needed to talk. He told Mark to go back to work, but that he will be watching him for erratic behavior.

Mark had just met with another *border bully*. Border Bullies are on the edge of your comfort zone, and they wait for you to get brave enough to go beyond the border of your comfort zone. When you do venture out, they try to bully you back. Why? Because it shakes up their life when you become brave, and they do not like it. They challenge everyone who decides to do something great with their life. Mark was told about these people by the Retired Chief. They don't want you to move ahead. Yeah, Mark knew the Senior Chief meant well, but he would not let the Senior Chief entice him to change his mind, steal his dream, or beat him down. Mark left the Senior Chief's office feeling like he made a mistake—was the Senior Chief right? *Was he making a mistake?* On the other hand, something inside said that his mind was made up and no one would take this opportunity from him. Every border bully causes you to reevaluate your commitment to the dream, we all have moments of doubt, discouragement and we have to recommit to the dream. Sometimes these people who mean well actually have a good point, so we should always take into account what they say especially if what we are doing is unsafe, risky or financially devastating to our family.

One day while swimming at lunchtime, Mark noticed a fellow swimmer doing the crawl, and this guy had an incredible crawl stroke. He took about five very slow strokes and swam the length of the Olympic-size pool. He would twist his body from side to side, which caused the water to ripple up and down and he looked like a submarine's hydrodynamic signature. This guy was incredible, and Mark had to know what he did to make the crawl look so effortless.

When this guy got out of the pool, Mark went up to him and asked him how he learned to do the crawl like that. Arrogantly, he said, as if this was the most stupid question in the world, "I practiced." He then walked away. Mark knew he had the same body as this guy, he didn't have gills and fins, he was just a man, and that if this guy could learn to swim that well, then so could he.

That night he hit the bookstore and library and picked up some swimming books, and the one that got his attention was underwater filming of Mark Spitz doing the breaststroke (Mark Spitz won seven gold medals for swimming in the 1972 Munich Olympic Games). Of course, the book had many other strokes, but Mark was focused on passing the swim test, and the breaststroke allowed Mark to keep his head out of the water. Most importantly it was one of two strokes allowed for the swim test. Why? Because as a diver you cannot do the crawl stroke with scuba tanks on; you can only do the breaststroke and the sidestroke, and these are also resting strokes because you kick and glide and you can swim in the ocean for a longer period of time. Mark read the book, copied the book's description of the breaststroke and practiced it every time he went in the pool. He worked it, and worked it, and worked it some more. The key was to practice, just like that guy said. The proper breaststroke also helped to develop his chest and back muscles, which Mark really liked. This would pay off in meeting future physical requirements for Navy Dive School and EOD School.

Well, Mark had fears but continued to move toward them even though he was extremely nervous. He practiced for the physical training test and pushed himself very hard. One day while doing push-ups he heard a loud pop in his head and felt the muscles from his back shoulder blade area tense up and pull all the way up his neck to his forehead. This was so intense that he just hit the floor and lay there a while until he was able to get up and go to the medical clinic. They took an x-ray and said nothing was broken. They told him to take Motrin and come back in two weeks, oh, and don't exercise for two weeks. This was hard, since he knew he needed to be in shape for the physical training test. Push-ups were impossible, but he knew he had to pass the physical training test. For the next two weeks he rode his bike and did exercises that worked his legs but not his upper body.

This was another test for Mark—would he let an injury hold him back or postpone the test? *No way!* Motrin would have to be his friend the day of the physical training test. Mark heard all the positive, motivating words in the gym and on TV—like Nike's "Just do it", "no pain, no gain," "suck it up, deal with it, nothing great in life comes without sacrifice," and :you just have to push yourself beyond the pain." So that is what Mark decided to do. When the goal is small, the pain you will put up with is small, but when the goal is big, you will have to put up with more pain and sacrifice.

The test for Navy diver, Explosive Ordnance Disposal Technician, and SEALs were all done the same way. The main difference was that the SEALs needed faster run time and swim time to qualify.

The day of the test came, and there was a physical fitness tester from another base who came down to administer the physical training/swim test. Mark chose the EOD test, and there was his friend Matt trying out for the SEALs, so Mark and Matt tested together. Again, the only difference is that Matt had to complete a faster time in the run and swim.

On the morning of the physical training test, Mark was nervous, just like anyone who takes a test—we all want to pass and everyone fears failure. The test was set up so that the run is last and the swim test is first. If you fail the swim test, then you stop the whole test. But if you pass the swim test, you move on to the push-ups, pull-ups, sit-ups, and then the run with boots on. Mark knew that if he passed the swim test the rest would be downhill because he was more confident out of the water than in the water.

Mark got to the pool and was told to dress out and meet on the pool deck. He was scared. His future was in the balance that day. *Will he succeed or fail, will he sink or swim? Will this be another rejection, and will he walk off the pool as a failure?* Mark was ready, but his body was not. He went to the bathroom twice. This test literally scared the crap out of him. But Mark knew he had to give it his best shot.

This was Mark's moment of truth, and to increase the pressure, the local EOD team that responded to the bomb threat at his building came there to cheer him on. *WOW!* There was the tester and four EOD team members, and it was just Mark and Matt testing for the SEALs.

"Consult not your fears but your hopes and your dreams. Think not about your frustrations, but about your unfulfilled potential. Concern yourself not with what you tried and failed in, but with what it is still possible for you to do." – Pope John XXIII

Mark knew he must pass this swimming test or there would be no diving and demolition future, he would lose face with these guys, and he would have to return to the Senior Chief and tell him he failed. *No way!* This cannot happen, this will not happen, and quitting was not an option. They would have to fail Mark, because Mark was determined to give it his all, with no holding back. He was determined to pass. There were no other options but to face his fear and move on. Mark would not quit or say he would quit.

What Mark did not know was that when a person has a dream that is pulling at his heart, all the forces of nature come together to help make this dream become a reality, and he will not be denied.

Moving into the fear and going through and beyond that which you fear almost makes that fear go away. Fear only exists when you do not do what you fear. But once you rationalize the fear, break it down and analyze it, and you know what you must do, you put in the hard work and practice, and do it safely. Then the fear slowly diminishes. The fear does not go away. But once you are doing what you fear, it doesn't seem so fearful.

Well, Mark got into the water and did just like he had practiced at lunchtime for the past nine months. He swam the breaststroke with the best form he could and as fast as he could. Mark thought, "If I can pace myself with the other guy swimming to pass the SEALs time, then I will surely pass the EOD time." So he swam his best.

Mark passed the swim test with a score fast enough to get him into the U.S. Navy SEALs, and he was ecstatic. All the time he spent running, swimming at lunch, and exercising after work, sacrificing partying and going through the "Border Bullies" (the folks who don't want you to leave your comfort zone, as presented in *The Dream Giver* by Bruce Wilkinson) and his peers, who told him he was crazy, was now paying off.

Now all he had left was the push-ups, pull-ups, sit-ups, and a mile-and-a-half run in army boots. Mark knew he could pass all of these as long as his form was good.

When it was over the proctor told Mark he did well and that he scored high enough for any of the diving programs, but Mark was focused on more than U.S. Navy diver—he wanted to be a U.S. Navy EOD technician and blow things up—dive and do underwater demolition.

He was told that the test results would be forwarded on to Washington and that his orders for U.S. Navy Second Class Dive School would be on the way. This was the first step in the Explosive Ordnance Disposal pipeline—you must complete Dive School in order to dispose of underwater ordnance like torpedoes and mines. If you do not pass Dive School you cannot become an EOD technician.

Mark was flying high. No one knew that he had a fear of the water because he met all the criteria. Mark passed the swim test and was not reprimanded for his inability. Mark knew that he was not able to overcome the fear by himself—only through the hard work and prayer did he make it. By the Grace of God, good things happened to Mark.

When something new is invented, a new model car, a new jet aircraft, or a new rifle, there seems to be the following common steps to follow:

1. Develop a plan, blueprint, and a goal.
2. Make a prototype, a sample.
3. Test it; try it out to make sure it works; make adjustments.
4. Field test it and subject it to different environmental conditions.
5. Put it into production and let people use it and provide feedback for modifications.
6. Make modifications and improvements.

And so it is in overcoming a fear. Every fear has the following steps that must be completed in order to get over the fear:

1. The fear is there with or without a good reason; decide not to run away.
2. Decide to go beyond the fear; have a strong reason to face the fear, and make a step-by-step plan that allows you to take small, achievable steps.
3. Define what it is you are afraid of and what it feels like.

4. Face the fear and decide to pay the price (to do what you have to do).
5. Define the hazards—what is the worst that can happen? Find a solution.
6. Practice, watch others, learn from others, read books, watch videos.
7. Practice more; modify what you are doing wrong.

In Mark's case, he had the fear and didn't know why, but let the fear paralyze him, and he ran from what he feared. Mark then took Step 2—he decided to go beyond the fear, and he discovered that he had good reasons to face the fear. Some of the reasons were more money as a diver, better advancement opportunities, more excitement, and more recognition. So he made an exercise plan, planned the date to go to Dive School, and planned the price he would have to pay. He figured that the worst that could happen was that he would drown, so he went out and got a good life insurance policy just in case. The life insurance cost for an electronics technician was much lower than that for a diver or someone handling explosives.

Mark watched others at the pool, read books on swimming techniques, and practiced often. This was the key to his success. This was the first swim test Mark passed at the age of 29 (besides the boot camp swim test). When he took the aircrew swim test he had no plan, he was not reading books on swimming, or talking with others, and he was not practicing in the pool.

Mark did not have a working plan to pass the Boy Scouts, or aircrewman test. Desire is not enough. That is why he failed the test. He never read a swim book about how to do the strokes properly, he did not practice in the pool, and he just looked bad during the swim test and did not show confidence in the water. However, once he practiced in the pool, got input from the Navy divers and EOD, and practiced more with the new information, he was on the road to success and he looked confident. He had a "can-do attitude," even if on the inside he was not all that confident. Anyone who has a fear to overcome must have a plan of some kind and must practice, learn, and get better, and confidence will come in time.

Courage is needed in overcoming fear. If there was no such thing as fear, then there would be no such thing as courage. People think that courageous people have no fear, but this is just not true. They manage the fear, and instead of running away from the thing they fear, they run toward the thing they fear. Then we call them courageous, and people say they are fearless, and again this is not true.

A Medal of Honor recipient was once asked if he was afraid, and the man said, "It's a valid question—the difference between me and the other guys is that instead of running away from the things I feared like the others, I ran toward them. But I was still scared."

Because there is fear involved in achieving every dream and every great endeavor, fear will have to be faced the way Mark did it. We must overcome the fear with courage, or we will never do great things. We must overcome the fear of failure in order to invent new things, and overcome fear to speak in public, fight for what is right, or fight against the oppressors in life and those who want to steal our freedoms.

Every dream has a number of borders, zones where we are uncomfortable, a challenge we did not expect that we must break through. And going through these borders increases our resolve and increases the will to succeed, to persevere, and to overcome.

This is one of the reasons many people never achieve their dreams. They think that a great dream should not have a border of fear, and if it is the right dream, they think that it should be easy and without challenges. This is wrong thinking! To achieve a dream, there is a price to pay, and the price will not always be the same for everyone, even for the same dream. If it is a small dream, then there will be a small price, but if it is a big dream, it will have a much bigger price to pay.

Mark passed the test and was now ready for a new chapter in his life. But with each new phase of the dream there will be more challenges, more risk, and more fears. This is why the struggle is great for a great dream. If it was too easy you would not gain the strength and resolve to push on when the going gets tough.

"Anything I've ever done that ultimately was worthwhile initially scared me to death." – Betty Bender

Fear can hold us back from moving forward in our life, furthering our education, and pursuing the things in life we were designed to accomplish. As Henry David Thoreau wrote in *Walden* in 1854, "The mass of men lead lives of quiet desperation." They want to do great things but have never taken the steps to move forward into the wall of fear and toward their dreams. Or if they have moved to the wall of fear and felt the resistance, they thought they should not have fear if this was the right dream and they back off, or they postpone the dream because they think it is not the right time.

"People think I'm disciplined. It is not discipline. It is devotion. There is a great difference." – Luciano Pavarotti

It was now the first step of many future days in the pool and in the open ocean, many days during which Mark would have to face his fear and have the courage to move forward.

The orders finally came in and Mark was scheduled for Dive School in Panama City, Florida. Fear is almost always in front of you and not behind you. You always fear the things in front of you, the things you have not done yet. Once you do the thing you fear, most often the fear diminishes. Mark's new fear was passing Dive School and now, with orders in hand, he was ready to leave for that very place. The next month he left for the Navy Diving and Salvage Training Center in Panama City, Florida.

CHAPTER 5

PAIN IS WEAKNESS LEAVING THE BODY

Mark checked into the Navy Diving and Salvage Training Center, in Panama City, Florida. He knew from the day he arrived at Navy Dive School that there was a difference in these Navy divers from the regular sailors, and he wanted to be a part of this. He made a personal promise to never quit and to do his best in school, because he wanted to be a part of these divers and wanted them to be a part of his life, too. They were strong, professional, with a "can-do attitude," and even a bit cocky and arrogant.

The instructors were proud of who they were, where they dove, and the jobs they did to get them recognized as the finest divers in the world. They were proud of who they were, how tough they were, and had a "can-do attitude." This meant that they wanted their students to rank among the best, too, so if the wannabe's didn't meet the grade, those students would be dropped from the class. The reason for dropping could be for academics, physical ability, or for a bad attitude.

One of the factors that helped Mark to stick to his goal and keep repeating to himself, "Just get through today, one more day, just one more day," was the fact that the U.S. Navy diver instructors had a great love for the water, an excitement and love for their job, and were enthusiastic in sharing their knowledge and producing the finest divers in the world from their Navy Dive School.

The motto of the Navy diver community is, "We dive the world over." Because divers may be assigned in any part of the world, their environment will vary as widely as water conditions vary: cold, muddy waters where underwater tasks can be completed by "feel" only, or warm, tropical waters clear enough to perform underwater photography with visibility of over 50 feet.

Mark arrived at Dive School two weeks before class started, because the EOD team told him that "if you get there early you will check into "X" Division where you can do physical training every morning and acclimatize to the humidity of Panama City, Florida, plus you will work somewhere in the school and learn about diving before class starts." You can remove a lot of the fears of the unknown when you can get adjusted to the buildings, tools, and instructors before you are put into a class.

While in "X" Division you were required to participate in physical fitness every morning with the other students and were exercising with the student divers in class. The big difference is that the other divers are already in a class and have a dedicated set of instructors. The students are evaluated every morning when they do physical training. When you are in "X" Division you are exercised the same but you are not evaluated and cannot be dropped, so you are allowed to exercise at a hard pace. This gave Mark a two-week head start to get in shape. Physical training lasted from 7:00 a.m. to 9:00 a.m. Then you showered, dressed, and went to class if you were a student. But in "X" Division you are assigned duty somewhere in the school.

Mark was lucky and was assigned to the Dive Locker. He inventoried all the scuba gear and tools, and was at the swimming pool. He saw the students in training; he jammed the scuba bottles with air, learned all the names of diving tools and where they were stored, saw the students get in trouble, heard the instructors' pool rules, and of course heard the students getting their butts chewed. This was a blessing for Mark because he learned the routine, saw other classes in the pool, swam at lunch, and learned how to maintain the diving equipment. Mark became more comfortable with the diving, the equipment, and the school process.

As you know, Navy divers are subjected to swimming, running, calisthenics, intense classroom instruction, and the instructors push the students to test their determination, their ability to learn fast, and their ability to overcome fear. One day someone complained of sore muscles and pain. The instructor said, "Pain is weakness leaving the body." So pain was good, pain was normal, pain increases the diver's endurance.

Now Mark was in a position to change his life, and he feared the change that he wanted. The fight was internal, and the voices were right between his ears. The voices in his head were like two dogs fighting. One dog was happy, positive, and excited. The other dog was nervous, scared, and negative.

The question is, "When the dogs fought which dog would win?"

The answer was easy, "The one he fed."

As long as he fed the dog that was positive, he would make it through school. But the minute he fed the other dog, he got scared, nervous, and had butterflies in his stomach.

Mark knew that school would be a physical challenge, and the classroom intensity would make it an academic challenge as well, but the biggest challenge was to keep up the positive self-talk, to stay courageous and push against the wall of fear and get over it, around it, or under it, and—above all—to never quit.

CHAPTER 6

DEFEATING THE WALL OF FEAR

Would Mark ever overcome the fear of the water? Can anyone overcome the fear of anything, or will that fear follow them all the days of their life?

Well, Mark said he always had butterflies in his stomach when he got near the water. Maybe it is a respect for the danger and power of the water. You see, our bodies are made up of about 70% water. We must drink water or we will die in about three days. Water is needed for life. However, water has the power to destroy an island or a coastal city. It can sink a ship at sea and it can drown a diver underwater if they do not have air in about five minutes or less.

Yes, Mark respected the power of the water, and he moved toward his goal in spite of the fear in order to achieve his goal. His goal was to become a Navy diver and then to be an EOD Master Blaster in the U.S. Navy. *Hoo Yah!* No, Mark did not lose the fear; he just learned how to control it by rationally reviewing the facts.

"What are the facts," you ask? Well, there were hundreds of people who loved the water and have no fear, and there are many divers who graduate every year from Dive School and nothing bad happened to them. There are surfers and snorkelers who every day hit the water; there are fishermen all over the world making their living in and out of the water. If they can do it with or without fear, then all Mark would have to do is copy what they did.

If you know what they know and you do what they do, you can have what they have. It was simple in theory, but the theory never removed the inner fear that something may go wrong in executing this simple but scary plan.

The fear was never based on seeing anyone drown, and Mark never personally knew anyone who drowned. The truth was that the fear was never based on anything factual. It was all an emotional fear, fear of the unknown. Fear of what could happen, may happen, might happen—but there was no reason to believe it *would* happen. Mark realized that the fear of failing Dive School, of losing face by dropping out or quitting, was greater now than the fear of the water.

Peer pressure sometimes is so strong that you will do things you are scared to do or do not want to do. Remember when you were with your friends and they double-dog dared you to do something? Many children in the big city have gangs pressure them to do things they do not want to do.

Hopefully, you are hanging around people who pressure you to become a better person and not get into trouble. Mark was pressured to do better, physically, and to go beyond his comfort zone. This pressure was actually good for Mark.

Sometimes in life you may have more than one fear or embarrassment fighting against each other. You may have a fear of heights, but your girlfriend or boyfriend wants to go on a Ferris wheel or walk on a high bridge. You don't want to say you are scared, so you go anyway. This was very true with Mark. The fear of quitting and losing face outweighed the fear of the water. The fear and embarrassment of showing fear in front of his peers, when they were not afraid, was a greater embarrassment than the fear that was holding him back from getting in water over his head. The fact was that if others can move forward and do anything in the water, all Mark had to do was to push himself beyond the wall of fear and into the world they were in. So he knew he had to push himself.

The only question was whether Mark could get to the wall, face the fear, and then go through the wall or over the wall and enjoy the other side. Well, as long as Mark did not quit and did not walk away he had a chance to make it through to graduation day. The opportunity to prove himself was getting closer every day.

Mark would show up to Dive School early in the morning dressed in Underwater Demolition Team (UDT) shorts and a blue and gold shirt (reversible T-shirt; blue was for students, and gold was for the instructors) He would do physical training with the class for two hours. He would shower, dress, and go to classroom studies in diving medicine, underwater cutting and welding, diving tables, physical injuries, emergency procedures, and different styles of diving rigs—from scuba to surface-supplied air such as the Mark V, Mark 12, and Jack Browne. At About 3:00 p.m. it was back into the pool, and the drills started. This is where the confidence training started and tested him up and beyond the wall of fear.

The pool was a big Olympic-sized pool that was 15 feet deep at the deep end. Navy Student divers (wannabes) spend a minimum of one hour a day in the water after classroom training. However, during scuba training they will spend the whole day poolside, with no classroom time. They will be assembling the scuba gear, learning line-pull signals, putting divers in the water, and practicing water entry and exiting. And when you mess up you will be doing push-ups, sit-ups, flutter kicks, or whatever the instructors can think up.

Swimming every day for an hour after classroom assignments was routine. But what they put you through was not a routine swim day! Over-and-unders, breath-holding relays, swimming the backstroke in a circle in the pool with a diving mask full of water, treading water, and of course drown-proofing. Every day was different—each time in the water was designed to increase the divers' confidence and strength and to reduce the fear of the water.

On the first day, they have the students go off the platform just like in boot camp. Again, Mark had to go off the platform! This time with more confidence!

Swimming in the pool is fun for most people, but what you did in the Dive School pool was very challenging. One day the instructors said you were going to do relay races, so they broke the class in half and they said, "Here are the rules: Half of each team goes to the shallow end and half goes to the deep end of an Olympic-size pool with a 15-foot deep end. You are to swim underwater to the other end of the pool and tag a teammate. That person will swim back to the other end of the pool underwater and tag the next teammate. This process will continue until the entire team has completed the relay." But here was the kicker—if you come up for air you must get out of the pool, do 25 push-ups and get back into the pool where you came up for air, and continue underwater. If you come up again you must get out and again do 25 push-ups and then continue from where you got out.

Mark thought that if he couldn't hold his breath underwater and got out, he would hardly be able to hold his breath after the exhaustion of 25 push-ups and continue. He knew he would have to make it in one try or black out underwater trying.

When it was Mark's turn he took a deep breath, pushed off of the end of the pool, and glided as far as he could. When he started to slow down he kicked and tried to keep his body straight and as hydrodynamic as possible so he could go far on a single stroke. He continued this until he was getting tired and out of breath; he could feel pressure on his throat to breathe out and get air, but he could not, he held it in, and kicked again. The pressure on his throat was pulsing, his body wanted air, and the spasms were getting worse. He knew that if he got out of the pool it would hurt the team and he would be so tired from push-ups that he would not be able to go far on a single breath. He kicked again and again. Then he could see the black line on the pool floor getting closer—this meant he was getting into the shallow end of the pool. The spasms were getting stronger, and he let out some air to reduce the pressure on his throat. His lungs were starting to burn. He kicked again and pulled with his arms. Again the spasms were stronger, and he let more air out, he knew it was make it or pass out. And then as he looked forward, the end of the pool was blurry but in sight. He kicked and pulled as air was leaking out. He reached the end and thrust his head out of the water, gasped for air, reached for the relay partner, and tagged him. *He did it!! Wow! He really did it.* He never swam the length of the pool underwater before, and he did it. Mark was congratulated by the others and he said to them, "You can do it, too—just don't stop swimming."

This was the beginning of Mark's extending the boundary of his comfort zone, ignoring his fear, and gaining confidence in the water. This was slowly becoming fun for Mark.

One of the pool games the divers played was "Over and Under." Half the class swam the width of the pool on the surface and the other half swam toward them underwater. Once they reached the side of the pool they turned around and swam toward each other again and this time the under team swam over and the over team swam under. This challenged their breath-holding and confidence in the water. Most of all, it gave the instructor a chance to evaluate the students in a controlled environment. They could see the strong swimmers and the weak ones who will need to be dropped from training.

One of the biggest challenges for Mark, but something that increased his confidence, was walking the bottom of the pool holding your breath. This was another relay race, and the class was divided into two teams. Half of each team was standing on the side of the pool at the 15-ft. deep end of the pool, and the other half was standing at the shallow 4-ft. end.

The task was to hold half of a Mark V weight belt (approximate weight is 42 lbs.), jump in at the deep end, walk the bottom of the pool to the shallow end, and hand off the weight belt to the other team member on the shallow end. That person, in turn, would walk it to the deep end and swim to the surface and hand it to the next man. This would continue until all of the team members swam both ways.

So there were two relay teams, and all team members had to cross twice underwater to win. Each person had to go from the deep end to the shallow end and then from the shallow end to the deep end on a single breath hold. Again, in this race, if you needed air, you left the weight belt on the bottom, got out, and did 25 push-ups.

Mark didn't know who won, but he knew that he had to push himself as he completed each leg, because his body was in spasms for want of air. The instructors said the students would be able to do it, and Mark believed the instructors and did it. That gave him confidence in himself and in his instructors. The instructors always pushed the students but never told them to do things they could not do. The fear was in the mind but not in the real task at hand. The limitations are in the mind, and until you push yourself, or are pushed by others, your belief in your own ability cannot grow.

These were remarkable days in Mark's life, because while he was always ready to get out of the water when they said training was done, his forcing himself to increase his comfort zone and to go beyond the wall of fear was something that taught him many things. No classroom training or self-talk, or even a positive mental attitude, would help him to overcome the fear. It is always, in the doing that great changes are made in people. The action of rewriting the memory pathways of the brain made all the difference—those pathways now say, "It *can* be done, you *can* do this, fear is not real..." You can push yourself to the point of making new limits, and as the instructors told Mark many times, "adapt, improvise, and overcome."

The underwater walking and the over-and-under swim tests seemed challenging, but they helped the instructors weed out the wannabes from those who really wanted to be divers. They also instilled confidence in the students and added to their trust in the instructors.

Everything you did in Dive School was done with a dive partner. You sat together, ate together, and even went to the bathroom together. This was to get you used to the fact that when you dive in the open ocean, under a ship at night, or in muddy water, you never do so alone. Your dive partner is the one who can save you in a time of trouble. You are taught to never leave your dive buddy, to care for each other, and to never get separated.

One day the instructor had the class dress out for scuba diving, in twin tanks and a BC (buoyancy compensator), weight belt, fins, and mask. Your buddy helped you dress out and vice versa. Once the entire class was in the water, they had you tread water, because in the middle of the ocean, of course, there is no side of the pool to hold on to.

If you did hold on to the side of the pool you were asked in not-so-nice terms, "What is your problem? Do you want to quit? Do you want to get out of the pool? There is no side of the pool in the ocean, so get away from my side of the pool."

Mark was swimming with his buddy and the instructor said, "Inflate your BC so you are buoyant. You are going to swim the backstroke with your buddy. But we are going to swim the backstroke with a mask full of water. Sometimes you will have your mask knocked off and sometimes your mask may leak, so get used to water going in your nose."

Mark thought this was harassment but learned later that this was a valuable lesson for diving in the open ocean.

The instructor, with a deep commanding voice, said, "Okay, take your mask off and fill it full of water, put it on, and begin the backstroke in a circle in the deep end of the pool. So the entire class, holding on to their buddy's tank straps, swam in a circle with a mask full of water. Remember that everything you do, all day, is with your buddy at an arm's length from you. They teach you to not be selfish, and to never, never leave a fellow diver behind and without air.

Now water has this funny way of seeking its own level and since your nose has two holes the water has a tendency to drain into your nose. So the minute you put the mask on and lay back you have this constant trickle of water into your nose, down the back of your throat past the gag reflex. And you either swallow the water or spit it out.

This was the most uncomfortable feeling for Mark, and the other students, too. However, Mark just let the water trickle in his nose. The smell of chlorine, and the taste of chlorine, burned as it went down the nasal passages. Mark could hear the instructors telling the students to fill their masks with more water and put them back on (some had taken them off), and he could hear the other students coughing and gagging. Mark just kept letting the water drain and then spit it out of his mouth.

Once the mask was clear of water it became more comfortable. Mark didn't say a word; he just kept swimming. Most of the instructors were too busy telling the other students that were gagging and coughing to fill their masks again, so they overlooked Mark. As long as the other students had the instructors' attention they didn't focus on him. (The students had a saying in school: "If you're not cheating, you're not trying.") Mark never really understood that saying. He thought cheating was wrong. But as time went on he learned that getting through each day was the goal and that some days you do whatever it takes, especially during physical training. When the instructor is not looking you cheat on the push-ups and take a break.

This pool training taught the divers how to control themselves and how to avoid panicking when a given situation happens. The situation of a flooding mask or a lost mask can happen in the open ocean, and as a diver in the ocean you don't have the option to get out or to get another mask. You must finish the dive and the mission.

Once Mark got out of the pool he had very clean sinuses and his breathing was very comfortable. He didn't recommend this nasal irrigation technique, but it was effective nonetheless.

The preceding text illustrates just two of the events on different days that slowly prepared Mark, a wannabe Navy diver, for the testing that would come in week five of Second Class Dive School. The more often Mark was around the water and the more he had to push himself to try new things, the more the fear subsided. The fear never went away, but he was able to control his reaction to the fear.

Mark kept saying to himself, "One day at a time, one day at a time, just one more day to go." This was all he could think about. Anything more would make the whole effort seem overwhelming.

The question is, "How do you eat an elephant?" Answer: A bite at a time. So Mark just focused on passing that day's events. He would look only to the day at hand. I think it is the same way for mothers—if they knew how many dirty diapers they would have to change, they might be discouraged about having a baby, but if you just change them as they come and don't count them, then it is manageable.

"Just one more day in the pool," "just one more day in the classroom," "just another day to go," he'd tell himself.

One day they had a small accident. One of the scuba divers panicked in the water and bolted to the surface of the pool, and he pulled his buddy with him. They both were embolized from surfacing so fast, and they both went to the hyperbaric chamber. So for that afternoon the class was two divers short, and they both were in the chamber getting treated.

Mark was really set back at lunch because the divers in the hyperbaric chamber were his friends. He said to himself, "We are here to be taught, not to be hurt—this is training." Mark thought back to his swimming lessons as a child. He was in class to be taught to swim, not to be fearful and leave the class not knowing how to swim. So why are people getting hurt and not learning to be good divers?

The accident was a good reminder to Mark to pay attention in class and learn to control his emotions, especially his fears. Fear is not an option when your life and the life of your dive buddy is on the line. When you are breathing compressed air at depth and you swim to the surface you must breathe the air out. If you don't, the air will expand in your lungs and your lungs will rupture or an air bubble will grow and block blood flow to the brain or other organs.

The guy who panicked was dropped from training; divers are taught that *you must never leave your buddy*, you must never let go of your air, and you must be trusted underwater. The worst thing that can happen to you as a diver is for people to fear diving with you. Once a diver panics and hurts himself or others, it is hard to trust them in the water. In this case, the panicked diver should have never left his dive buddy and should never have pulled the other diver off the bottom. He needed to control the fear and not panic, and if there was a problem he needed to communicate this to his buddy and then they would both go to the surface in a controlled manner.

This is a lesson to take through all of life. Having a buddy who will watch your back is very rare in this world. This is taught to all U.S. Navy divers, Explosive Ordnance Disposal Technicians, and SEALs. Never leave a buddy behind, and never leave a buddy down range.

They drove this lesson home in Dive School. When you started school they paired everyone up so everyone had a dive buddy. You took your buddy everywhere you went and he took you everywhere he went. You stayed within an arm's reach in the pool, on the side of the pool, and so on. If they ever caught you separated, you were punished and had to wear a rope about four inches in diameter that was tied with a loop on both ends to fit over the divers' shoulders and about a two-foot piece between the loops for separation. The loops were around your buddy and the other was around you. You wore it to class, to the pool, to the bathroom, and so on. This way everyone knew you lost your buddy, and it drove home the importance of checking on your buddy.

The Bible has a verse where Cain asks God if he is his brother's keeper. Well in Dive School you definitely *are* your brother's keeper.

Well, Navy divers always think of their buddy diver, and all Navy divers as their brothers. They will give their life for their fellow Navy divers. Even years later after they get out of the Navy they still have this mentality in their morals and values for life.

Part of the Navy Dive School plan for teaching divers (http://www.netc.navy.mil) includes the following:

> **Mission**: Train qualified candidates into proficient Military Divers in support of Naval, Joint, and Allied operations.
>
> **Command Philosophy**: Accomplish the mission, take care of the troops, and do the right thing.
>
> **Guiding Principles**:
>
> - Make a difference every day.
> - Honor your oath.
> - Be forthright and truthful.
> - Do your best.
> - Create an environment to succeed.
> - Keep a steady strain.
> - Know yourself, know your troops, know your boss.
> - Respect the dignity of everyone.
> - Have fun with confidence.

You may ask what keeping a steady strain means. When a diver has surface-supplied air, the air in a hose goes to the diver's helmet. The hose and line are used to communicate to the surface with line-pull signals. Two pulls on the line mean I am moving away and give me slack. Four pulls on the line mean I am coming up. So if the line is too tight, the diver has to fight to move and swim, but if it is too loose and he pulls to give signals, the surface will not feel them. So keeping a steady strain means to have the right tension on the hose.

So, too, is it with your fears. If you have too much fear you may panic and hurt yourself or others, and if you do not have enough fear to respect the water you may be complacent and get hurt. Mark's fear was translated into respect for the water—in the beginning he wanted to run from the water, and now he was moving toward what he feared, with caution and respect. Fear was not an option, and if Mark let fear become an option he would have chosen the easy way out. Instead, he chose the hard path to overcome his fears.

Mark never quit, and when the instructors got in his face and asked him if he wanted to quit, Mark always said no. Mark said to himself that he would never admit failure or quit. He told himself that the instructors would have to fail him—*they* would have to make the decision that he did not have what it takes. He knew if he did what he was told, put in the extra time, studied at night, and put out a good effort that he would make it. So for 13 weeks he did just that, one day at a time. The day he knew he would make it is when they took a class graduation picture and he was in it.

Mark stood in line with the other graduating divers on graduation day and he knew at that moment that he had overcome his fear and he had the approval of the dive instructors. He never spoke of his fears of the water to the other divers or the instructors. He figured if they knew he had a weakness they might focus on it and pressure him into quitting. Mark wanted a fair chance to pass the school. He didn't kiss butt to make it, and he didn't have any high connections in the front office. He knew that *he* put in the time and effort, *he* did the physical training, and *he* passed the test in the water and underwater to make it. Only three-fifths of the class was standing on that day. The rest didn't make it.

"Never talk defeat. Use words like hope, belief, faith, victory."
– Norman Vincent Peale

If you persist in pursuing your dream, all the forces of nature come together to make it happen. You must have belief, speak positively, and when you are confronted with a problem or a challenge you must not ask why. You must ask how.

Don't ask, "Why is this happening to me? Why am I having a hard time?" You have to ask, "How do I get past this obstacle, how do I go over it, around it, how do I solve this challenge and move on?" It's been said that if you have to fall down, try to fall forward, because that way you are gaining ground. It is not that you will have a bad day or fail a test. This will happen; it is what you do about it, it's your attitude during it, and the work you do to get past it. Mark, "with the grace of God," made it to graduation day and was pinned with the Second Class Diver pin.

CHAPTER 7

SHOULD WE HAVE FEAR?

If we didn't have fear, if we were not afraid, if we did not fear anything, we wouldn't survive very long. We'd be just like little children that will walk in the street or crawl off the edge of the stairs because they don't know the danger of gravity, acceleration, and suddenly stopping the human body.

If we did not have fear, we would try to pet a snake, step off a cliff, or put our hands in a fire. The purpose of fear is to make us stop and think about the possible consequences of our action and to warn us that what we are about to do could be hazardous to our health or life. Fear is a part of us to ensure self-preservation. Throughout history those who listened to their fears and feared the right things survived and passed this education on to their children and grandchildren. It may even have been passed down as a good trait and a response taught by our relatives to be aware of certain situations, such as when confronted by a wild animal. In that circumstance we become scared and either back down from the situation or pick up a stick or rock to defend ourselves. These traits and responses have been beneficial over time to ensure the survival of the human race and the family tree. Many times, unfortunately, our caring parents have taught us to fear the things they fear.

Most people in this civilized society ignore the fight-or-flight response or do not feel it as often as our great-grandfathers probably did. They feel secure and comfortable in their environment. When they leave the city to go to Africa on vacation in the wild, they still have the feeling of fear, though, and it is far from being outdated. This fear response is normal and part of not only human behavior but animal behavior as well.

Today we see this more and more, with extreme sports and reality TV shows, on which people voluntarily push themselves to break various records and push themselves to overcome their limits every day.

We continue to push aside this fight-or-flight fear response—we ignore it or we deal with it and control it. Today we are jumping out of planes, scuba diving, landing on the moon, living in space—all that was impossible a hundred years ago. These achievements and sporting events were unacceptable either socially or from a mental stability point of view, not to mention that people didn't have time or resources to make such activities possible. How many times have you said, "Those kids are crazy" or "That reality show on TV is crazy—I would never do that…"? Yet we keep on watching. Some events that we are scared to try ourselves we watch others do to see them overcome their fear and press on, and we confront our fears vicariously through these shows, movies, and courageous stuntmen. I have no interest in going rock climbing, but I enjoy watching others climb in areas that I would be afraid to climb.

Today we are bungee jumping, hang gliding, parachuting, diving with sharks, rounding up snakes, bear wrestling, and cliff climbing. We are diving deeper, finding sunken ships, splitting atoms—and we're building space stations in space. These were the dreams of people and considered science fiction 150 years ago. Yet we have gone past our fears and taken calculated risks to make these dreams a reality.

Does that mean today we are not as scared as those people 150 years ago? No. We may not be attacked by a wild animal when we cross town, but we still have a fear of walking down an alley at night, and we still worry about a carjacking, terrorist attack, or car accident. The fears are still out there, but they just take different forms, and we must be alert to them just as people who lived 200 or 2,000 years ago were alert to their fears. So our fear should protect us from dangers just as it has years ago. It is when we ignore the fear or ignore a situation that it can turn dangerous, or God forbid we stop listening to the little voice inside that says, "Something is not right in this situation."

Most of us have never been exposed to the black plague or been exposed to lepers, but when we hear someone talk about it we get a fearful feeling. Many of us have not been bitten by a snake or a spider but will jump back when we see them in the wild. We do not have to experience the bite of a poisonous snake in order to react to the presence of a snake as if our life were in danger.

Many people have never experienced a plane crash, yet they have a fear of flying. Many people also have never experienced any mishap whatsoever on an airplane but now fear flying after the airplanes crashed into the World Trade Center's twin towers on September 11, 2001. People cancelled flights and airlines lost business because people feared their flight would be the next hijacked plane. Anticipating an event can be as fear-inducing as actually experiencing the feared event.

Have you ever watched a scary movie and found your hands sweating, your heart beating faster, or have a friend reflexively scream at the actors to get out of the room, not open the door, or to run away? Emotions are high, and yet we as viewers are facing no real danger at all. The same is true of anticipating a fearful situation. We can have the same fear response from anticipation, just as if we were actually in the dangerous situation.

This ability to anticipate dangers has been an evolutionary benefit. When people in Kansas smell rain or feel the wind change and seek the storm cellar, they have a better chance of making it through the storm than those who ignore the anticipatory fear.

CHAPTER 8

FEAR TRAINING

A re we trained to be fearful? When we were children our mothers told us things that instilled fear into us so that we would avoid dangerous things and situations.

Things like the following were said to us as warnings:

- Don't touch the iron—it's hot.
- Look both ways before you cross the street.
- Put on your seat belt.
- Don't do that, or you'll break your neck.
- Don't go in the woods, or, the monsters will get you.
- Don't play with BB-guns, or you'll shoot your eye out.
- Don't touch the stove—it's hot.
- Don't sit on the toilet seat, or you'll get herpes.
- Don't play with snakes, or you'll get bitten.
- Put that stick down—do you want to put someone's eye out?
- Stay off the railroad tracks, or you'll get hit by a train.
- Don't go in the basement, or the boogie man will get you.
- Don't go swimming alone, or you'll drown.
- Get off the garage roof, do you want to fall and break your neck?
- Never get into a car with a stranger.
- Don't talk to strangers.

And the list goes on. Part of the fear we feel is evolutionary, but some fears come from scary stories, terrible pictures, e-mails, and YouTube videos. We may see more fearful things on the Internet in one year than our ancestors saw in a lifetime.

Conditioning is why some people fear spiders, snakes, dogs, heights, guns, fast cars, big government, water, explosives, and so on. Because of an event in our childhood, or something we saw in the movies, or on TV, we have been "taught" to have certain fears.

People may fear spiders or snakes because they were bitten as a child. But now it is a conditioned response, and when they see a spider or snake they have a flashback to the event that was fearful and they get scared as if the event were happening in the present. They will even pass this fear on to their children, who will fear these things because of their mother's or father's reactions to the particular event. Many people have a fear of dogs and may have been bitten by a dog as a child. Then 10 years later they may encounter a very nice dog but still get scared, and in their brain (specifically, the amygdala) they associate the sight of a dog with the pain of the bite.

Mark feared the water, and in his brain he connected the smell of chlorine with the fear of the water. Years later he would get scared and nervous from the smell of chlorine. Even the smell of bleach when doing laundry would create panic in him and he would have a flashback to the swimming pool event when he was a child.

Many times in war, soldiers will have a very close bond to those with whom they served. They experienced the same fears and near-death situations and have an inexplicable connection with these people. They have a common link, and that link is the war stories and the hazardous situations they experienced together.

Many veterans have flashbacks to those events years later. It can be the sound of a helicopter overhead, the explosions heard on the Fourth of July, the smell of gunpowder, or even the sight of a jungle, a desert, or a military vehicle. Because their fear is so real in their minds and in their bodies, many veterans refrain from talking about their experiences for many years. Some may never talk about these events.

It is said that the soldiers and sailors who never saw battle have a lot of war stories to tell, but the ones who really experienced it don't speak of those events or tell war stories. Funny how that works…

Phobias are generally caused by some event recorded in the mind by the amygdala and hippocampus (parts of the brain) and labeled as a deadly or dangerous event; thus, whenever a specific situation is approached again the body reacts as if the event were really happening in the present.

What is the amygdala? It is an almond-shaped group of brain cells (neurons) located in the medial temporal lobes of the brain. It plays a key role in processing emotions like fear, anger, and pleasure.

Phobias are more often than not linked to the amygdala, an area of the brain located behind the pituitary gland in the limbic system. When the fear or aggression response is initiated, the amygdala may trigger the release of hormones into the body to put the human body into an "alert" state in which they are ready to move, run, fight, and so on. This defensive "alert" state and response is generally referred to in psychology as the fight-or-flight response.

It is possible for an individual to develop a phobia over virtually anything. The name of a phobia generally contains a Greek or Latin word for what the patient fears plus the suffix "phobia" ("fear" in Greek). So aqua phobia (or hydrophobia) would be a phobia of *aqua* ("water" in Latin) or a fear of water (*hydro* is water in Greek).

Phobias are a common form of anxiety disorder. An American study by the National Institute of Mental Health (NIMH) found that between 8.7% and 18.1% of Americans suffer from phobias. Broken down by age and gender, the study found that phobias were the most common mental illness among women in all age groups and the second most common illness among men older than 25.

Treatment consists in replacing the memory and reaction to the perceived fearful or deadly event with something more realistic and rational. In reality most phobias are irrational in that the subconscious association causes far more fear than is warranted based on the actual danger of the stimulus; a person with hydrophobia or aqua phobia may admit that their physiological arousal is irrational and overly reactive, but this insight alone does not cure the phobia.

CHAPTER 9

WHAT ARE SOME OF THE COMMON FEARS?

According to surveys, some of the most common fears are of ghosts, the existence of evil powers, cockroaches, spiders, snakes, heights, water, enclosed spaces, tunnels and bridges, needles, social rejection, failure, physical examinations, and public speaking. In an innovative test of what people fear the most, Bill Tancer analyzed the most frequent online search queries that involved the phrase, "fear of." This follows the assumption that people tend to seek information on the issues that concern them the most. His top ten list of fears consisted of flying, heights, clowns, intimacy, death, rejection, people, snakes, success, and driving.

Another common fear is the fear of public speaking. Many people are comfortable speaking inside a room, one-on-one, or with friends, but when it comes to public speaking, the fear of others watching and judging their performance is too great for some people. Another common fear can be of perceived pain, or of someone damaging a person. Fear of pain in a situation brings flinching or cringing.

In a 2005 Gallup poll (in the United States), a national sample of adolescents between the ages of 13 and 15 was asked what they feared the most. The question was open-ended, and participants were able to say whatever they wanted. The most frequently cited fear (mentioned by

8% of the teens) was terrorism. The top ten fears were, in order: terrorist attacks, spiders, death, being a failure, war, heights, criminal or gang violence, being alone, the future, and nuclear war.

People develop specific fears as a result of learning. This has been studied in psychology as fear conditioning, beginning with John B. Watson's Little Albert experiment in 1920. In this study, an 11-month-old boy was conditioned to fear a white rat in the laboratory. The fear became generalized to include other white, furry objects. In the real world, fear can be acquired by a frightening traumatic accident. For example, if a child falls into a well and struggles to get out, he or she may develop a fear of wells, heights (acrophobia), enclosed spaces (claustrophobia), or water (aqua phobia or hydrophobia).

Over the years there have been many studies of the brain that investigated which areas in the brain are affected by fear. When looking at these areas, especially the amygdala, it was proposed that a person learns to fear regardless of whether they themselves have experienced trauma or if they have observed the fear in others. In a study completed by Andreas Olsson, Katherine I. Nearing, and Elizabeth A. Phelps, the amygdala was affected both when subjects observed someone else being submitted to an aversive event, knowing that the same treatment awaited themselves, and when subjects were subsequently placed in a fear-provoking situation. This suggests that fear can develop in both conditions, not just simply from personal history.

Although fear is learned, the capacity to fear is part of human nature. Many studies have found that certain fears (e.g., animals, heights, public speaking) are much more common than others (e.g., flowers, clouds, clowns). These fears are also easier to induce in the laboratory. This phenomenon is known as preparedness. Because early humans who were quick to fear dangerous situations were more likely to survive and reproduce, preparedness is theorized to be a genetic effect that is the result of natural selection.

The experience of fear is affected by historical and cultural influences. For example, in the early twentieth century, many Americans feared polio, a disease that cripples the body part it affects, leaving that body part immobilized for the rest of one's life. There are also consistent cross-cultural differences in how people respond to fear. Display rules, norms about appropriate modes of expressing emotions, affect how likely people are to show the facial expression of fear and other emotions. Experiencing fear every now and then is a normal part of life. But living with chronic fear can be both physically and emotionally debilitating.

Common types of fear and phobias

Abandonment

Aging or the elderly

Bad breath

Bad odors

Bathing, washing, or cleaning

Bats

Being alone

Being bad, corrupt, evil, defective

Being controlled by others

Being deprived

Being harmed

Being incapable

Being laughed at

Being looked at or stared at

Being of no value, worthless

Being out of mobile phone contact

Becoming too cold

Being touched

Being unloved

Being useless

Blood

Bridges

Bright colors

Broken glass

Belly buttons

Cats

Change

Chemicals

Childbirth or pregnancy

Clowns

Color yellow

Computers/ Learning new technologies

Conflict

Contracting a disease

Crossing the road

Crowds

Darkness

Dead fish

Death and/or the dead

Defeat

Dentists and dental procedures

Diminishment, decline

Disease

Dogs

Dolls

Doing wrong

Driving

Duty

Eating fish

England or English culture, etc.

Engulfment

Everything
Failure
Falling
Friday the 13th
Flowers
Fire
Foreigners or extraterrestrials
Germs, contamination or dirt
Germans
God
Growing old or aging
Ghosts and phantoms
Grave, or fear of being placed in
    a grave while still alive
Hair
Having an injury
Having no escape and being
    closed in
Hell
Heaven
Heat
Heights
Hurting others
Holes
Home surroundings and
    household appliances
Hospitals
Ignorance
Incompetence
Incorrect decisions
Injury
Insecurity
Intimacy
Invasion of boundaries
Isolation

Itching
Lack leaving a safe place
Limitation
Loneliness
Long words
Looking stupid
Loss of connection
Losing money
Losing things
Loud sounds
Love
Marriage, commitment
Making decisions
Material loss
Meaninglessness
Medications
Mental illness or the mentally ill
Missing out
Money
Mortgage
Music
Newness, novelty
Needles or injections
Night
No identity
Obesity
Open spaces or of being in
    public places
One's photograph taken
Pain
People or the company of people
People or social situations
Personal insignificance
Phone

Places or events where escape is
  impossible
Pope
Possessiveness
Poverty
Public speaking
Radioactivity or X-rays
Rain
Reluctance of making or taking
  phone calls
Risk taking
Rejection
Relationships
Responsibility
Self
Self-exposure
Self-expression
Selfishness
Selling
Separation
Sexual abuse
Sharp or pointed objects
Shyness
Sleep

Snakes
Spiders
Strangers, foreigners, or aliens
Stupid people
Success
Sunlight
Support, guidance
Swallowing
Technology
The number 666
The number 4
The number 13
The sea, or fear of being in
  the ocean
Thunder and lightning
Trees, forests or wood
Truth
Unknown
Vomiting
Vulnerability
Water
Weapons, specifically firearms
Workplace
Work or functioning

CHAPTER 10

HOW DO YOU OVERCOME FEAR?

S tudies have shown that rats with damaged amygdala will walk right up to cats. Most of us would not have an operation to remove the amygdala, although it may be a way to remove fear. So scientists are exploring other ways to overcome fear. Mark had the fear of water, but as he continued to face his fear over time, and with exposure to the water with no adverse effects, he slowly built confidence and began to rationally determine that the fear of drowning was unfounded and unnecessary. He practiced in the pool and pushed his limits of breath-holding and solving problems in the water, which in turn increased his confidence. He then was able to relax and gain skill and confidence in swimming. Thus, over time the fear response decreased.

Fear extinction involves creating a conditioned response that counters the conditioned fear response. While studies situate the amygdala as the location of fear memories formed by conditioning, scientists theorize that fear-extinction memories form in the amygdala but then are transferred to the medial prefrontal cortex (MPFC) for storage. The new memory created by fear extinction resides in the MPFC and attempts to override the fear memory triggered in the amygdala.

Most behavioral therapies for fear extinction focus on exposure. For instance, therapy for a person with a fear of snakes might involve

89

visiting a snake farm repeatedly and taking small steps toward touching one. First, the person might get within 10 feet of the snake and see that nothing terrible happens. Then he might get within five feet of the snake. When nothing terrible happens within five feet of the snake, he might get close enough to touch it. This process continues until new, fear-extinction memories are formed. These new memories say, "Snakes are not going to harm you" and serve to contradict the fear of snakes that lives in the amygdala. The fear still exists, but the idea is to override it with the new memory.

What steps can you take to overcome your fear?

1. **Face your fears:**
   a. Look back in your life and figure out what scared you.
   b. When was the first time you felt this fear?
   c. Identify what makes you scared, and what you feel when you are scared.
   d. Ask yourself what the worst that could happen to you is, and what you can do to prevent it from happening.
   e. Some fears you will just have to face head-on.
   f. Basically, find out what you fear and what you can do to ease the fear.

2. **It starts with a dream:**
   a. Have the end in sight.
   b. What does success look like to you?
   c. How would you like to see yourself reacting to this fear?
   d. Picture in your mind how you would react with courage.
   e. Once you desire the results more than what you fear, you will find a way to achieve it.

3. **Have a goal:**
   a. Break the fear down into small pieces. An example: Fear of water.
      i. Get in the water three times a week.
      ii. Get books on swimming.

      iii. Watch videos of swimmers.

      iv. Take swimming classes.

  b. Set deadlines to achieve each of these goals.

  c. Study the thing you fear.

  d. Be strong; keep moving forward toward the goal, and chart your progress.

  e. Moving toward your goal does not mean taking uncalculated risks, doing unsafe things, or doing anything illegal.

4. Have a plan:

  a. If it's a Big Dream, you must have a big plan.

  b. Talk to others who overcame this fear and ask how they did it. Take notes.

  c. Create a plan to incrementally test yourself by getting closer to what you fear. Revisit Mark's plan in Chapter 3 for getting into EOD School. That's a small plan, but it's the basic form any plan will take.

  d. Create a desire and plan for success that is greater than the fear. Mark had a plan to become a Navy diver, and he first planned to get in shape.

  e. Anything you do physically will require you to be in shape for that activity.

  f. Mark studied diving, talked with divers, studied the entrance test, and trained with the EOD and Navy divers.

5. Be persistent:

  a. You have heard the saying, "Quitters never win, and winners never quit." Find someone who does not have this fear and ask them how they feel when they are in this situation. Copy their thinking and mannerisms.

  b. Resolve to never quit.

  c. Take some action on the plan every day, no matter how small. Keep moving closer to the goal.

  d. Anything you truly want in life you must work hard to achieve, so resolve to work hard.

6. **Take it one day at a time:**
   a. Each day will have its problems, and you must solve those problems and not worry about tomorrow.
   b. You can rest one day but never quit. This may be the one fact that you must embrace if the fear is big.
   c. How do you eat an elephant? One bite at a time! Mark had to do his best—one day at a time. He put in 10 hours of doing his best, and then went home, did the homework, and prepared for the next day.

7. **Enjoy the process, laugh, keep a sense of humor, smile (you cannot fear what you love):**
   a. When you love what you do, it is no longer work— it becomes fun.
   b. Love the thing you fear, learn about it, see others enjoying it, and the fear will slowly decrease. It may not go away completely, but it will decrease.
   c. Fear is a warning that you are doing something dangerous or risky, so be alert and cautious. Diving is dangerous, and the fear is real, but also manageable with proper education and training. Learn about it, study it, and love it.
   d. It is hard to be scared and nervous when you are laughing; make light of the situation and laugh whenever possible.

8. **Help others in the process—team work:**
   a. Whenever you work toward something you fear or help others to get over their fear, you end up helping yourself, too. Remember that you will always push harder when others motivate you and when you motivate others.
   b. You must work with others and have help from others for education, training, support, and setting a plan in motion. Use each other as motivators. Mark had a friend preparing for the SEALs and they exercised and ran together. It seemed that when one was up the other was not and they helped each other to stay motivated.

c. A dive team, an EOD team, a sales team, a sports team, or even your family can help give you moral support, encouragement, and praise your achievements. This may be the only team cheering for you.

d. Your family members can be your best support in helping you achieve big dreams. When you are down, tired, or ready to quit, they can give words of encouragement to motivate you.

e. "A rising tide lifts all ships." Share your success and encourage others to follow.

CHAPTER 11

HOW DOES A PERSON FACE THE FEAR?

Fear is what tells us to be cautious. Fear tells us we need to be more alert than normal. Fear gets us ready to move forward or move backward, to take the field or to hide. Fear is what allows people to develop courage and to do great things that others fear to do. Fear does not separate the men from the boys, because all feel fear. Fear is what allows boys to take to the field and to become men and girls to become women. Overcoming your fears and moving forward separates the men from the boys and the girls from the women. Sometimes the emotions tell us to be afraid, but when we recognize the fear (not in a life or death situation where we have to react fast) and logically look at the situation, the right thinking will allow us to overrule the emotions and fear and work on a way to get past them.

"The fear, is worse than the pain."
– Shannon Bahr

Fear is normal! Fear is part of the equation for success. Without fear, courage would not exist, and without courage, heroes would not exist. You must have fear, and the overcoming of fear by having courage produces people who are called heroes. In their time of courage they knew that fear was not an option. They had to overcome the fear and complete a courageous act in spite of the fear.

"Fear is the main source of superstition, and one of the main sources of cruelty. To conquer fear is the beginning of wisdom."
– Bertrand Russell

Fear is what makes men plan ahead. Fear is what keeps us alive in the jungle of Vietnam, the desert of the Persian Gulf region, and in the ocean miles from land. Fear heightens the senses and makes us focus on the events around us. Fear is what makes us pay attention to the details and be alert when we do new things that scare the pants off us.

Fear keeps you alive and alert on the flight deck of an aircraft carrier as aircraft land at 150 mph and when you dive in the Red Triangle with the great white sharks. However, if we let fear paralyze us we will never face our fears with courage and do great things in our life—or live our dreams.

Fear is what motivates Christians to obey God's laws and respect God's words. Fear of the great leaders and tyrants made people obey and respect them.

It's not about doing something that scares you but about doing the right things with courage!

There are plenty of people in the world who do things that are scary, like being rude to people or scaring people just to put it on a video, stealing from stores because of the rush they get, damaging property, reckless driving, and so on. These may be scary things to do, but they are also *wrong* things to do.

Overcoming fear to rob a bank or swindle someone out of their money is not something that we are speaking of. In this book we are concerned with overcoming fears to do the *right* things in life—to serve others, to save the lives of others, and to achieve goals and dreams of great value. We're also concerned with pushing yourself to become better and developing yourself. This book is about the right way to create the courage to overcome the fear and do great things in your life.

There are many stories of people who have sacrificed their lives for their friends. The soldier who carries his wounded buddy to safety, the young man who jumps on a grenade to save his fellow soldiers, the missionary nurses and doctors who go to other countries to help the people fight disease. There are divers who risk their lives to dive to great depths to recover a critical piece of equipment for their country or to repair a damaged ship so it can safely return to dry dock for repairs. Young men and women who go to war are scared that they will never come back. And yet they go, willingly.

Mark dreamed of doing something great with his life. But he needed to grow. First, he needed to have a direction. And the goal was to pass Second Class Navy Dive School. For Mark this was a big, big, BIG, challenge. He knew he would have to go beyond his fear and to hide the fear from the other students and the instructors. If they found out he was scared to get into the water it would blow his cover and he would be pressured into quitting.

Second, he would have to overcome the people who said he shouldn't do it and the instructors who always give you the chance to quit. The instructors pressure you to quit and ask you, "Do you want to get out of the pool?"—all the time knowing that if you get out that you will be dropped from class.

Third, he had to go beyond his comfort zone, and every day Mark was *way* out of his comfort zone. As a matter of fact, Mark developed a twitch in his right eye that lasted from week two in Dive School until the end of Dive School. Then it went away. Of course, Mark hid it from the instructors and other students. Fear and stress can cause involuntary bodily movements.

When you are on the journey toward your dreams, you must ignore everything around you that is negative and absorb the positive things that move you forward spiritually, physically, and mentally. It is amazing how the little things in life can derail you on the way to achieving your dreams.

Mark dropped all hobbies, partying, and book reading, except the *U.S. Navy Diving Manual.* This one manual is so important for a Navy diver, and it can mean the difference between life and death of a diver.

Mark will never forget his dive instructors. When he closes his eyes he can see them on the side of the pool, manning the side, watching out for their students' safety, teaching them about pain, and making them strong. They took sailors as they were and molded them, helping them to increase their belief in themselves and to increase their endurance well beyond what they thought they could do physically and mentally. They also expanded their ability to do what they were told and to do it without asking why—to follow instructions in the dark, in the mud, in the sand, and through the pain.

Mark dreamed of the day that he would have the chance to be the Red Diver, to put the hard hat on, and to go beyond his comfort zone and stand on the deep sea cage while they lowered him over the side of the ship into the water.

Mark can still hear them yell, "Hoo-Yah, Red Diver!" and when the dive was over, he remembers the feeling of standing on the deck and saying, "Red Diver on deck, Red Diver, OK!" all the time knowing you have done what less than 5% of the U.S. Navy sailors will ever do. Being in the top 5% is a feeling that no one will understand, and the feeling inside is a feeling no one can take away—"Hoo-Yah, Red Diver"—"Hoo-Yah U.S. Navy divers!"

Don't misunderstand—it is not about the great diver, or the great instructor. It's about the great mentors. These are men of steel; they were strong and were not afraid to get in the water with you and show you how it is done. They were not afraid to drop you from training if you were not trusted in the water. The instructors already proved themselves in the field, and now they were passing on to the new divers what they had learned.

The instructors would drop you for push-ups if you were doing the wrong thing and if you got caught doing the wrong things, then of course you had to pay. It takes strong people to not let you slide, to not look the other way, or to make life easier for you.

Instructors had the endurance to watch students languish in pain and do push-ups until some threw up their breakfast. Many instructors would say, "You will do push-ups until I get tired," (of course, *he* was not doing push-ups with the students, he was just saying: down, up, down, up...). Or the instructor would say, "Don't mind the pain. Pain is weakness leaving the body." During push-ups the instructors would ask the students if they wanted to rest; at first, the students fell for it and said, "Yes." So he would say, "Up." Of course, the up position for push-ups is the resting position. So with their arms extended holding their body weight up, they would (for what seemed eternity) rest until they were done resting. Then he would say, "Do you want to stop resting?" and of course the students would say, "Yes," so they would continue with more push-ups. *Little did the students know* that this was the way to build muscle. In five weeks, Mark was in the best shape of his life, with a hard body, and he felt like an invincible Navy diver.

Pain is part of growing up, pain is how muscles are made bigger, and it is pain that gives us endurance and a can-do attitude. Pain is part of the tradition of producing strong, disciplined Navy sailors, and discipline kept Mark alive on the flight deck. When Mark crossed the foul line, when aircraft were coming in at 150 mph, he was severely reprimanded in front of everyone on the flight deck, but after that day Mark got his act together and paid attention to the details. Mark learned how to prevent an ass-chewing and was extremely alert on the flight deck. Abuse, huh! Abuse is part of life, part of war, and part of becoming a man. Don't miss the point. Abuse, discipline, and pain are all different. Many people do not know what the difference is or where to draw the line.

Again, don't miss the lesson. It was not how strong Navy divers got, it was not how big they got, it was not even how educated they were—it was always about how great the mentors were, how much teaching, instructing, and love they put into their class. Mark never got it until

Graduation Day, when the instructors had to shake their hands and welcome them into the diving community. You could see in the eyes of the instructors that they had grown close to the divers in their class over a period of 13 weeks. They ran with the students, exercised with the students, and were responsible for the safety of the class through all the pain, the sweat, and the tears. They grew close to the students and were proud of the few that remained until Graduation Day.

The diving instructors saw the great advances that their students had to make in order for them to get through the 13 weeks, walk across the stage, and graduate. Mark was proud to go through this ceremony and would never forget it.

All the training and all the simulations in the world will never substitute for the real thing in time of need. Every bit of pain and every time you push beyond your comfort zone contributes to an increase in your confidence and marks out a level of battle that you will be able to go through without flinching. Many soldiers and sailors lose their lives for their country because they flinched, retreated, or froze in the time of confrontation.

Pain is weakness leaving the body, and pain in training will mean the difference in battle when you need to push yourself and get the job done. U.S. Navy divers complete the mission, however long it takes and however long they must work. Mark never saw such a strong-willed group of sailors. The Navy divers are the best of the U.S. Navy. They are academically, physically, and mentally strong, and they push themselves past the pain, past their comfort zone, and past what many would call the point of quitting.

The 25 that started class 13 weeks earlier were now down to 15 graduates. Forty percent dropped out from Mark's class. The ones that were left were the 15 divers who endured all the harassment and pain that the Navy could give, and the graduating divers felt good about who they became. Endurance and pain are part of a growing and maturing human being.

Mark looks back with love on these mentors and instructors for their hard "I'm going to kick your ass, you're going to wish you were never born" attitude, an attitude that made him pursue the dream and push through the pain to the accomplishments and to a point at which he could truly love the person he was becoming. These mentors are giants in his mind and are the kinds of men all young boys need to grow and model themselves after as they become men.

Mentors are hard to come by. I see many people who promise to help you, but they have one hand in your pocket stealing you blind as they say, "Look to the dream," and they manipulate you and your friends for their greedy motives and greedy gains.

"My mentor said, 'Let's go do it, not You go do it.' How powerful when someone says, 'Let's!'" – Jim Rohn

---

All mentors are not created equal. And some who call themselves mentors are not interested in seeing you rise above them. Some will hold you down if you get too close to them. It can be a game of egos, and people who act like this are the people who give mentors a bad name. You may know them as con artists, manipulators, and users. When you get taken by one of these, many times you will never trust anyone again, or at least anyone in that field of business.

"A lot of people have gone farther than they thought they could because someone else thought they could."
– Zig Ziglar

Navy diving instructors are men with real goals of being the best and teaching you to be the best. They do it so the U.S. Navy will have the best divers. Mark is very proud to have had mentors like this in his life and recognizes how valuable they were to him.

They took Mark in 13 weeks from a sailor filled with fears to a sailor who became a U.S. Navy Second Class Diver. He was a hard-hat qualified, MK-12, Superlight, Jack Browne, underwater welder and scuba diver, a proficient swimmer, and a man who was proud of his life.

"Hoo-Yah! Red Diver," "Hoo-Yah! Navy Diving Instructors!" Why do they say Red Diver, Yellow Diver, and so on? The diver's air hose is a certain color. Red Diver has a red hose. Yellow Diver has a yellow hose. When you have multiple divers in the water and they all have the same color hose, how can you tell them apart? If Red Diver says I need more air, topside will know which valve to turn. All they have to do is look at the color and trace it back to the valve. When the diver comes out of the water, the diving supervisor wants to know if his diver is okay and expects the diver to say, "Red Diver on deck, Red Diver okay." So the diver is now called by the color of the air hose.

Navy divers focus on completing the mission with a can-do attitude. The question is always, "How can we get it done"? The question is never, "Why do we need to get it done?" Quitting is never an option. Maybe we go back to the drawing board, regroup, and make a new plan, but we never quit.

Why do some quit Dive School? And why is it so important not to quit? Those who quit didn't have the resolve, or the "I will try until I succeed, I will persevere until I win, and I will continue until I graduate" attitude!

Uncontrolled fear drives people to quit. Fear, just like love, is a decision that starts inside a person. When fear is replaced with love, the person will relax and view the situation from a different vantage point. Gandhi had a love for his country and his cause. His love was so great that he was able to go beyond the fear to starve himself, to peacefully protest, and to be put in jail. He had the courage to go beyond the fear of taking on the opposition to his cause. Fear holds many people back from persisting. Why is this? Some do not have a strong enough dream—some say when they start, "Well, if things get bad I'll just quit!" And sure enough, things will get bad, painful, frustrating, and hard, so the self-fulfilling prophecy comes true. Fear can cause people to make the decision to quit.

What is a quitter? What are the traits of those who quit?

Merriam-Webster's Collegiate Dictionary-11th Edition gives this definition of "quit:"

Transitive verb
1: *to make full payment of :pay up<quit a debt>*
2: *to set free :relieve, release<quit oneself of fear>*
3: *conduct, acquit <the youths quit themselves like men>*
4a: *to depart from or out of b: to leave the company of*
    c: give up 1 <quit a job> d: give up 2<quit smoking>

Intransitive verb
1: *to cease normal, expected, or necessary action <the*
    engine quit>
2: *to give up employment*
3 *to admit defeat: give up*

We as a nation are becoming weak, from our leaders down to the man on the street with his hand out looking for a free meal ticket.

Where is the pride that was instilled into our forefathers to say things like, "Give me liberty or give me death"? Many people will not pursue a cause to their death. Many people in this country will lose face, risk embarrassment, and do not even care. They will push a child or woman out of the way to get what they want. I saw a man steal a woman's purse on TV. What ever happened to men holding the door open for a lady? And how can a person who treats women badly look into a mirror—these are not the traits of a real man. The police motto is to "protect and serve." This should be the motto for all citizens in the world. When I was a child, I was taught to hold a door open for a woman, to help carry groceries to someone's car, to share my food, and to say please and thank you. You know, these are the things we were taught in kindergarten. But how many people carry these habits into their adult lives and how many people pass these ideas on to their children and grandchildren?

We as a nation will stay strong by working at it, exercising our morals, values, and physical bodies to endure more and to grow. Like the retired Chief said, if you want to move up and become a Chief you have to do better in every part of your life. You have to stand out in the crowd. How many of us set high goals to achieve?

Mark set high goals and took advantage of every opportunity that came his way. It was not easy, but it was the right thing to do. We as a nation expect the government to help us get ahead, and when we do not get ahead like we think we should, we want to blame others for our lack of achievement when it was only our laziness and lack of planning that held us back.

Mark only got stronger by exercising and pushing himself beyond his known limits. I think this nation may have to experience hard times to grow stronger. We as a nation want too many government handouts and we have too many freeloaders that are pulling the nation down and raising the national debt. We need "men of steel and velvet," as the author Aubrey Adeline has stated. There must be a balance between working hard with strong values and determination on the one hand and having compassion and peace both as leaders and as citizens on the other. We need people with high morals and values like our forefathers had. We need church leaders to hold fast to God's teachings and not bend to the world's desires for money, fame, and "political correctness."

When things get bad, such as in a natural disaster, or when a ship is in distress, our people feel confident that our military can help. That is why we have Navy divers who can help when there is an accident in the water. They will fix the problem, because they have the determination not to quit until the problem has been solved. Why do Navy divers have this "never quit" and "can-do" attitude when most civilians will not give their "all" in life or for their country? Many of us walk past situations where we can help, but we turn our heads and say, "It's none of my business; it's not my fight." People quit because in our school systems, our sports, and our culture we are becoming weak and lazy. However, this does not have to be the future, and I pray to God that America will always have God's blessing.

Navy divers never quit and have a high resolve and determination because they require it in the screening out process. A very high level of physical fitness is required, and because they want the best of the Navy, the top 5%, being a Navy diver is not for all people. The standards are high and must be kept high. These men are physically and mentally strong—with a can-do attitude—they never quit on a mission and always work as a team. This type of attitude needs to flow over into all people in America if we want to stay strong. We need to have the pride to say, "I do not need a handout. I will get off my butt and work, I will do my part and I will never quit. I will never quit on the American Dream and I will work on America's team to make America better."

Mark thought of the day he was taught to never quit and to never give up. During pool training the instructors bound the legs and hands of the divers-in-training and put them in the water to teach them to not fear the water and to teach them that they will not drown, even when they cannot use their hands and feet. This was a test to see how the students reacted and to show the instructors that the students will not panic and that they can learn survival swimming. What does a diver do when he is in the ocean with no ladder to get out and he gets tired? Answer: drown proofing.

Divers are taught that you can survive, you can swim, you can get air, and you will not drown. The lesson is to never quit, never give up, and never give in to fear!

Mark had entered Dive School, and after 13 weeks of training, excitement, perseverance, and love, he passed U.S. Navy Second-Class Dive School.

Mark loved what he was doing and was becoming stronger than his fear. He became a Navy diver, much to the surprise of his mother and his family. If you have a fear, replace the fear with love and the fear cannot exist.

Fear and love cannot exist at the same time. Mark could not fear the water and love to swim, he could not love to be a diver but be scared to put his face underwater. He could not fear drowning and allow himself to be tested in the water for extended breath holds and swimming to exhaustion. Either love conquers or fear conquers. And Mark slowly forgot the fears and pursued the love and the dream to be a Navy diver.

"Love to be real, it must cost—it must hurt—it must empty us of self."
– Mother Teresa

Don't misunderstand and think that all fear disappears. That is not the case. Fear is telling you to be cautious—it's telling you to be prepared for fight or flight. But the fear is like a dashboard light in an automobile that says the wiper fluid is low. The light tells you that there is something to be concerned about, but it does not stop you from driving the car and continuing on your journey. You must be more concerned about getting to your destination than you are about what the dashboard light indicates needs attention (in this case, a non-essential feature, wiper fluid), so you continue driving.

So it was with Mark with the smell of chlorine. Mark still gets butterflies in his stomach, but it is just a dashboard light for wiper fluid. It's not a light for low oil, which he'd have to take care of immediately, and it does not stop him from jumping in the deep end of the pool.

There are many other fears in life that stop many people from doing the things they want to do in life. Let's look at some of them now.

Fear of Rejection

Fear of rejection is a fear of failure or rejection in the presence of others. You are afraid of how people will think of you, so you are afraid to act, say, or do something foolish. Many people are afraid to have different opinions on life or the world than other people do, and they do not want others to reject them because of their opinions. Many people will become quiet in a crowd if others have opinions that differ from theirs. They may not express their opinions when at family events because they fear rejection from family members. It takes courage to have your own opinions on life and to stand tall and not cave in to others because you fear they will reject you.

Fear of Change

Some people are so comfortable in their life that they will not change jobs, move to a better home, or move to another state to have a better lifestyle. They are afraid to take a vacation to another country, go on an ocean cruise, break a tradition, or change a bad habit.

For many people, change is a big wall that they cannot get over. They are so comfortable in their life that they feel fear when they contemplate change and are unable to plan a better life, make the hard choices to change habits, try different foods, or experience other people's lifestyles or cultures. Again, it takes courage to step out of your comfort zone and do something different. Change is part of life, and many people enjoy trying new things, going on vacations, and doing new things. If you are one of these people, make small changes in your life that will have a positive result. Then do things that you can build on and try bigger things, such as traveling outside of your comfort zone for longer periods of time, and you will see that life and the world are exciting.

Fear of Success

Fear of success is the fear that holds many people back from achieving their dreams in life. Many people see that success can be a curse; success will make you arrogant, nasty, and a snob. They fear having money, because "it is harder for a rich man to get to heaven." They fear success because they may have to talk in front of others, may be asked to lead others, will be in the upper 5% of people, and will not be able to blend into the crowd. Eighty percent of people are followers, and to move into the twenty percent scares them. Many feel inadequate—that they don't deserve to achieve good things—and also suffer guilt when they do better than others, or better than expected.

Overcoming this fear will require doing a lot of self-talk, examining your conscience, and taking the time to focus on a plan, as discussed earlier, to remove the fear. Many people create a comfort zone that they do not want to get out of. They are a good employee; they do not have to or want to make decisions as a business owner themselves. They do not want to research investments and take the chance of risking what they've saved, or even part of it, in order to become successful. They listen to others who talk them out of doing something risky that may ultimately make them a success in life.

It will take courage, planning, and hard work to overcome this fear. You will have to work around good and successful people so their habits will rub off on you. The best people want to work with the best people, and clearly the way to keep good people is to keep them around good and successful people. You will have to ensure success without fearing it, or sabotaging it. Part of your plan must be to hang around with those who will encourage you and motivate you to succeed.

The confidence you will need is belief in your potential and yourself. If you see world-class potential in yourself, you'll put in the effort and never quit. If you don't see the potential, you may quit without putting in the effort and you'll sabotage the performance. Great performance always follows the belief in yourself.

Fear of Flying!

Fear of flying is very real for some people, and it is no joke to them. Many people think of the many pictures and videos of plane crashes and allow this thinking to grab them so much that their palms get sweaty, their knees start shaking, their heart races, and the feelings are so intense that they cannot even board a plane or sit comfortably during a flight. Many people know that flying is statistically safer than driving in a car, but the fear of heights, and the fear of leaving the ground scares the shit out of some of the bravest, burliest men.

Knowing of a plane crash, which usually kills all on board, can take over their rational thinking about the fact that thousands of flights take off and land safely every day. Their worries and fears grab them around the neck like a nutcracker on a New Mexico pecan.

They exaggerate their fear and worries, just as Mark did with the fear of water and drowning. The truth is that flying becomes safer and safer every year. Millions of people fly daily to their destinations. In fact, the lifetime odds of dying in a flying accident are one in 20,000 compared with one in 100 for an auto accident and one in 5 from heart disease (according to 2001 statistics).

About 20 million people in the United States suffer from some form of flying fear, ranging from a little anxiety to super fears (called aviophobia), and that will stop people from flying at any cost. Some have panic attacks when scrunched into a full plane.

Even when they experience a safe flight, that may not calm their fears. Those who actually board the plane and land safely at their destination might view the experience as lucky in an otherwise risky situation. When they get off of an airplane they want to kiss the ground, as if they just narrowly escaped losing their life.

Many flyers who must travel by air often attempt to push down their fears with sedatives or alcohol, but no matter how much they try, the fear may still be there.

Fear of Loss

Fear of loss can take many forms in life. It can be the fear of losing our material possessions, our career, our status, our property, our wealth, our salary, our health, our family members, our girlfriend or boyfriend, our spouse, our home, or our lifestyle. The fear comes because we have an attachment to the item that is at risk. Without such an attachment there would be no fear of loss. We have become attached to these things over time.

The fear of loss can caused many people to freeze within their current lifestyle. They stay at a job they don't like, live in a house they have grown to hate, and even live in a city or town they don't enjoy—all the time wishing they would move, change jobs, or live a different lifestyle. People have grown attached to the things in their lives and their lifestyle. So to pursue something different might mean relinquishing all the material things they have come to know. Because of this fear of loss, some people choose to put their dreams perpetually on hold; they do not pursue a better job, move to a different location, travel, or make new friends.

This is very illogical and comes about as a by-product of being too entrenched in our physical world. The reason why it's illogical is because everything in our lives, except our consciousness, will pass away. We were born into this world as ourselves, with our consciousness—no money, no possessions, nothing. We only have a fear of loss because it took time, money, and work to acquire these things. Thus, we feel we will suffer a loss if we let them go. When we die, we will lose everything and bring with us only our consciousness, our spirit or soul, and hopefully a history of our good deeds and actions.

So how do we overcome the fear of loss? We must first have a full understanding and realization that we fear loss only because we are holding on to things that we do not want to lose. We have to realize that we can do without these things and that life will still go on. We do not need a TV in every room and a big house for retirement when we only need a one- or two-bedroom residence. We need to know life goes on without the girlfriend or boyfriend. Only then will the fear and thoughts of loss diminish.

Don't misunderstand, though. Some of these things give us pleasure and make life easier, so we will keep these things. However, if you do not want the fear of loss, then you must cut the ties or come to the conclusion that these things can come and go and you will not throw a fit. Instead of concerning ourselves with what we have, we know that we cannot take these things with us beyond our death. Then, suddenly, it doesn't matter what we have in our lives—what truly matters is how we are living our lives.

Think about the day when you are going to die. Would you rather look back at having spent your life holding on to things that you can't carry with you after death or look back at how you have passionately and fervently lived out your dreams? Start by releasing your attachment to the things in your life. That's when you will start making better decisions for yourself and your life, devoid of fear.

Fear of loss can only be present when we are thinking of holding on to things, controlling these things. Everything we have acquired since birth will be taken away at our death. We are only stewards of the things for a short period of time. We are judged, not by how much we have acquired, but what kind of a steward we have been. Love life without holding so tightly to material things and the fear of loss will disappear.

Fear of Terrorism

In our world we are seeing more terrorism and acts of suicide that kill innocent people. These innocent victims are no threat to the people committing the homicidal acts. The reality of so-called "suicide bombers" causes people to have a fear of terrorism. I personally do not fear terrorism as much as I fear the loss of freedom. I think people who fear terrorism really are fearing the loss of life, liberty, and the pursuit of happiness. When someone takes their life away early, they have stolen the life of the innocent. They have stolen the opportunity for liberty and the chance to achieve their goals and dreams in life. They have stolen this innocent person's chance to pursue happiness. The victims have been robbed of the basic, inalienable freedoms given by God. I do not fear terrorism, but I do fear the loss of freedom and my God-given rights. However, some may fear terrorism and avoid places that may be targets for terrorist attacks, such as airplanes, tall buildings, embassies, and government buildings.

"It is not what we do that makes us holy, but the love with which we do it." – St. Thérèse de Lisieux

---

Most people will admit that they have a fear. Even if the fear is small. Some people may go through their whole life and never face the fear; they may avoid it or run from it. If you should choose to face the fear it will take courage, planning, and practice to overcome it. So be prepared for a challenge and to struggle against adversity.

Most of us have a fear of something in our life and our fears can cover every area of life—mental, emotional, physical, even spiritual. If we are really honest with ourselves, most of us, if not all of us, will recognize that we have one or more of these fears. Overcoming our fears gives enormous stress relief. So the question becomes, "How do we overcome our fears?"

Many people go to a trained counselor for help to overcome their fears. They experience relief and usually have a plan to act on to systematically work on understanding the causes of their fears. To overcome many types of fear, it is helpful to understand the basic mechanism of fear.

Fear is an emotion. It's an experience that is very deep and personal to most people, and sometimes we cannot explain why we have the fear. There are three parts to fear: a behavioral part, a physical part, and a mental part.

"I am convinced that life is 10% what happens to me and 90% how I react to it." – Charles R. Swindoll

---

There is an avoidance behavior that most people exhibit when placed in a life-threatening situation. We all have a fight-or-flight reaction to perceived danger. If the fear we experience is warning us of an imminent danger to ourselves, we will react without thinking. For example, if we are standing in a crosswalk, ready to cross the street, and the light changes and we step out in the street but the car coming doesn't see us, we react very quickly in order to avoid being hit by the car.

"The message is clear. It is not what is happening 'out there.' It is what is happening between your ears. It's your attitude that counts. Get your attitude right, and chances are dramatically higher that your economic condition will be good."
– Zig Ziglar

The physical part of fear will be one or more physical sensations in the body. These physical sensations might include shaking, a queasy stomach, rapid heartbeat, muscle tension, shallow and rapid breathing, and increased perspiration. We may also scream and run from the scene.

"It is not what happens to you but how you think about what happens to you that determines how you feel and react. It is not the world outside of you that dictates your circumstances or conditions. It is the world inside you that creates the conditions of your life." – Brian Tracy

---

The mental part of fear is specific to the situation. Our mind may go blank, it may think of past fears and situations, and we may have flashbacks to the past. We might not be able to think rationally, or we might think very quickly of ways to get out of the threatening situation. The mind takes over and we may lose control of bodily functions like our heartbeat increases, our breathing changes, sweating increases, and the pitch of our voice goes up.

When fear seizes us, it is in control. We lose control of our behavior, our physical reactions, and our mental functions. We are out of control. The only way that we will get the control back is to change our thinking on the inside about the thing we fear. We might need a counselor to help us get over the fear. We might need to slowly face what we fear and get more comfortable, or we might need to avoid what scares us, such as heights, wild animals, and the like. In the case of Mark, he created his own plan. He decided to get in shape, which led to incrementally getting in the water, swimming at lunch, and slowly working his way past the fear. He read about great swimmers, read about divers, and read the *U.S. Navy Diving Manual.* He changed the fear into interest—and then into excitement.

Mark passed U.S. Navy Second-Class Dive School and was now on his way to Explosive Ordnance Disposal (EOD) School in Indian Head, Maryland.

"If you change the way you look at things, the things you look at change." – Dr. Wayne Dyer

---

CHAPTER 12

---※═○═※---

WHAT IS FEAR?

According to the: Merriam-Webster's Collegiate Dictionary, 11th Edition:

fear (noun)
1a: an unpleasant often strong emotion caused by anticipation or awareness of danger

b (1): an instance of this emotion (2) :a state marked by this emotion

2: anxious concern :SOLICITUDE

3: profound reverence and awe especially toward God

A simple definition of fear is: *An anxious feeling caused by our anticipation of some real or imagined event or experience.*

In other words, fear is the feeling or condition of being frightened or afraid, *regardless of whether you have reason to be afraid or not.*

Your fear can come from something real or it can come from your imagination. Mark's fear was really of a nonexistent, unreal scenario, in which he saw himself dying. Had it been a fear of an actual dangerous situation, however, he would not have been able to overcome it. Mark anticipated and imagined drowning. He imagined the instructor not helping him, and he anticipated that he would never be able to swim. He also connected swimming with failure because he took two swimming classes and was not able to do the crawl. Thus, he avoided situations that put him near water in order to avoid the feelings of fear and failure.

"You have to find something that you love enough to be able to take risks, jump over the hurdles and break through the brick walls that are always going to be placed in front of you. If you don't have that kind of feeling for what it is you're doing, you'll stop at the first giant hurdle." – George Lucas

---

Fear comes about to help us escape danger—to run away from life-threatening situations. However, when it is something you must do, when it is a dream you must achieve, then fear is not an option, you must fight, and running away is not an option either.

The last chapter talked about the fight-or-flight response. If fear is blocking you from something you really want to accomplish, you must choose to run toward the fear and not away from the fear. But if it is a fire in a burning building and you are saving people, you must use caution and not reckless "courage." There has to be some thinking about personal safety, like putting on protective clothing, wearing supplied air packs, having knowledge of the structure of the building, and so on. There have been many courageous people who go to save someone and end up dying themselves.

Fear is part of a survival mechanism, and we feel fear so that we will not ignore a real danger and possibly get injured or killed. Fear is also a mechanism to trigger our reserve energy so that we can fight or have a clear enough mind to run away from or otherwise evade and hide from danger. It also fuels our ability to save our loved ones from danger. When we experience fear, our adrenal glands release adrenaline into the bloodstream, which causes a series of biological reactions in our body. It increases blood and oxygen flow to our muscles. It restricts blood flow to other areas, such as our stomach, to slow digestion. It dilates our pupils so we can better see things around us. When this happens, we have entered into "fight-or-flight" mode. This mode helps us to escape real physical danger. People will say they are scared when they have these feelings, and they feel very uncomfortable, but this is a normal reaction.

So, what is fear? Is it a feeling? Is it an uncontrollable biological change in the body producing fear? Is it a thought?

Some believe fear is a chain reaction in the brain that starts with a stressful situation (stimulus) and ends with the release of chemicals that cause a racing heart, fast breathing, energized muscles, panic, sweating, also known as the fight-or-flight response. The stimulus could be a snake, a police car's flashing lights in your rearview mirror, a classroom full of people waiting for you to speak, an approaching thunderstorm in Tornado Alley, or the repo man showing up at your front door. Or it could be the phone ringing that you think is the collection agency calling.

The brain is profoundly complex, with more than 100 billion nerve cells. The fear response is almost entirely autonomic: We don't consciously trigger it or even know what's going on until we feel the biological effects. Research has discovered that the following parts of the brain play central roles in the process of feeling fear:

- **Thalamus**—Sends sensory data from eyes, ears, mouth, and skin to the cerebral cortex.
- **Sensory cortex**—Interprets sensory data.
- **Hippocampus**—Processes stimuli to establish context; stores and retrieves conscious memories.
- **Amygdala**—Decodes emotions; determines possible threat; stores fear memories.
- **Hypothalamus**—Activates the fight-or-flight response.

CHAPTER 13

CREATING FEAR

The process of creating fear takes place in the brain and is entirely *unconscious*. Once it is determined that the stimulus may be dangerous and the fight-or-flight process may need to kick in, the body prepares by sending a flood of epinephrine, adrenaline, and dozens of other hormones into the bloodstream. These hormones cause the following changes in the body:

- Increase in heart rate and blood pressure
- Dilation of pupils in order to take in as much light as possible to sharpen the eyesight
- Constriction of veins in skin in order to send more blood to major muscle groups
- Focus of brain only on the big picture in order to determine where the threat is coming from
- Increase in blood glucose level
- Tensing of muscles, energized by adrenaline and glucose, which produces goose bumps—when tiny muscles attached to each hair on the surface of the skin tense up, the hairs are forced upright, pulling skin with them (also known as chicken skin)
- Shutting down of digestion and immune systems to allow more energy for emergency functions

These biological changes are intended to help you survive a dangerous situation by preparing you to either fight for your life or run for your life.

The fight-or-flight response, in particular, is an instinct that every animal possesses. Humans have the same reactions to fear as animals, but we have the ability to control our reaction by analyzing the situation and taking conscious control of the biological functions. So, instead of running from the car that pulls into the driveway that scares us, we look and see that it is only grandma coming to visit. We analyze the situation collect information, and control the biological functions by determining that what we initially saw as a threat is not a threat at all.

These biological reactions are helpful if we are *really* faced with a threat or real emergency for which we must have above-normal strength, speed, agility, and reaction time.

These bodily responses do not aid us when we are facing self-perceived dangers that do not result in any physical harm to us. If anything, we only become held back by these reactions.

Think about when people are afraid to board a plane, when they have stage fright, or when they become agitated from a high-stress incident. In these cases, you do not need lots of adrenaline pumping in your veins; what you need is to rationally look at the situation and deal with things logically and calmly. This is easier said than done, especially when you're ten years old and the water is over your head. The problem in the twenty-first century is that about 99% of the fear people experience today is from their mental perceptions, not physical danger. This includes fear of public speaking, fear of loss, fear of flying, fear of failure, fear of humiliation, phobias of things that pose no physical danger to you, and so on. This is mental fear, and this is the fear that prevents many people from taking risks to live their dreams and do great things with their lives.

As Mark felt fear, what it actually did was to give him an edge to perform harder, to try harder, and push harder. The fear increased adrenaline in his system, which actually helped with his strength, eyesight, and reaction time.

Real fear occurs in life-threatening situations like the following:

- Having your best friends tie bungee cords to your legs, and then saying you're a sissy if you do not jump, while you are standing on a bridge 110 feet above the river.
- The Army Airborne wannabe with a parachute on his back standing in the doorway of a plane looking out for the first time, all the while thinking that he can sit down and wait for the plane to land.

This kind of fear comes from placing yourself in *real* danger. Many people today are looking for an adrenaline rush by doing extreme sports and pushing the limits of speed, height, and their physical abilities.

"There is a time to take counsel of your fears, and there is a time to never listen to any fear." – George S. Patton

---

Fear is such a dastardly and invasive emotion. It holds us down from trying something new; it prevents us from taking action in our lives when action is needed and required. Usually there is no good reason other than not quite knowing what will happen. It is the darkness behind the basement door that we're so afraid to open; we just turn and walk away. Usually what actually happens is enjoyment, fun, or learning something new, but the best feeling is when you face your fear, run toward it, and break through the wall of fear. No one can tell you how this feels; you have to experience it firsthand. Mark felt this many times as he tried new things in the water and found out that if he pushed himself, he could do everything the diving instructors said and even more.

"You don't face your fears, you stand up to them."
– Anonymous

Now in our day and age, with what we call civilization, we do not always have physical dangers (unless you are in a war zone) So, how do you fight something you can't see—insecurity, depression, anxiety, PTSD, poor self-esteem, and terrorism? You don't. You just run away from it. We try and run away from so many things in our lives, including:

- Our terrible childhoods
- Our relationships
- Our responsibilities to others
- Our commitment to raise our children with thoughtfulness and attention
- Ourselves and the dreams that we truly want in our life

Try as we may, however, our attempts to run away often fail. Like Mark—he could run from the water, but he was always faced with water again and again as he lived his life. We learn that life doesn't really care what you want if you don't stop to face your fears. And God doesn't really care about your fears; he just cares that you do his will.

The following is adapted from a poem used in the TV show *Three's Company* (Season 4: "The Goodbye Guy." Author: Christmas Snow, 1979-80):

> You can run from pain,
> you can run from fear,
> you can run from crime on the street.
> You can run from your problems,
> you can run from your troubles,
> but you can't run away from your feet.

You can find the text at the following website:

http://www.connectingsingles.com/poem17303/chrissy-threes-company-season-4the-goodbye-guy.htm

Sure, you can get a divorce or end a relationship that seems to be going nowhere. You can drive your car on vacation because you're scared of getting on the plane. But was the problem the other person or the plane flight? Such problems simply reappear later on, in another relationship, with another person. If you avoid flying now, you may need to get home fast sometime when a loved one is sick. You will have to face your fear of flying again. You ran away from fear the first time, but it did little good because the problem remains.

"Courage is not the absence of fear, but rather the judgment that something else is more important than fear."
– Ambrose Redmoon

I suggest you start the process of putting fear aside. You have to face the wall of fear and you must find a way to break through it in your life. It is a process, and it will take time and courage. You have to learn to put aside your long-standing trust and commitment to your fearful thoughts and feelings. You have to look the fear in the face and say, "You will not beat me; I will adapt, improvise, and overcome you." You have to replace the thoughts of fear, the thoughts of "what if" and stop imagining what might happen or all the bad things that could happen. This is not an easy task and will take time. But once you break through a fear you will have one of the greatest feelings of achievement. Your self-esteem will soar. The best things in life take work, self-talk, time, and effort, and this is easily one of the best things you can do for yourself in your life. Living a fearless life is living a full life, open to potential, opportunity, and joy. You can do it, and I believe in you!

CHAPTER 14

IS FEAR PART OF SUCCESS?

There are eight key reasons why we should overcome fear in our life.

"Each time we face our fear, we gain strength, courage, and confidence in the doing." – Theodore Roosevelt

Why Overcome Fear?

1. There is a better life on the other side of the "wall of fear."
2. Fear prevents us from achieving our full potential.
3. Fear will follow you if you try to run away.
4. We never fully run away from fear.
5. You pass on the fear to others.
6. When you overcome one fear, you grow in the process, and this helps you overcome other fears.
7. Fear is all in our mind.
8. Fear is a waste of our energy.

"No passion so effectually robs the mind of all its powers of acting and reasoning as fear." – Edmund Burke

1. There is a better life on the other side of the "wall of fear."

When we fear something real or imagined we draw a line in the sand and we will not cross it. I will never allow myself to be near a clown; I will not go to high places; I will not sleep without a nightlight; I will not be embarrassed speaking in front of a crowd; or I will not get into the water. We set boundaries that we refuse to cross. I call these examples of the "wall of fear." This wall that we set up, even though it's not seen by others, is real to us. Mark set this wall up and avoided water, but circumstances put him in situations in which he had to face the wall.

When you turn from the wall of fear and go back to a safe place, life still goes on but you miss out on everything that is on the other side of the wall—all the opportunities that may come from going through the wall and from struggling past your fear.

When Mark broke through his wall of fear and became a Navy diver, a whole new world in the Navy opened up for him. Also, because he broke through his fear of the water, he gained the courage to break through other fears. He knew that most of the fear was only in his head and that the little voice that said "I'm scared. Don't do this" became the problem when he listened to it. It's important, however, to recognize that this voice *can* be the voice that stops you from doing something dangerous or stupid. But it can also stop you from going forward to learn new things and achieve your dreams.

2. Fear prevents us from achieving our full potential.

Fear will hold us back from doing great things in our life; it can paralyze us and stop us dead in our tracks. Many people work dead-end jobs when they really desire to move ahead. Fear in your life may be holding you back from being the great person that you were meant to be. Many people go to their grave with their unseen greatness still inside of them.

When you are overcome by fear, it stops you from moving to the higher levels of courage, acceptance, love, joy, peace, and enlightenment. As long as you are trapped in the land of fear and do not face that wall of fear, you cannot access those higher levels. You will not gain the confidence to move on to achieve your full potential. Giving in to fear in one situation in your life may allow you to take the easy way out of other fears in your life and allow a habit to develop. That's how a pattern of failure and avoidance of anything you fear is created. When you see the wall of fear in your life as a barrier, you will not look for the door or window to get through the wall. You will not look for a ladder to scale the wall or the pathway that others have taken to get around it, or the trench dug under the wall. When you never give up, you will look until you find a way over the "Wall of Fear."

Some people say that it's okay with them. They would rather back off in the face of fear and snuggle into the comfort zone where there is no fear. To them, this is the life that they look for—no danger, no threat, no anxiety. The government will take care of me. They are okay with not becoming their best. They are okay with taking the easy way out, being lazy, and looking for a handout. If that's the case with you, then what are you living for? What gets you excited about living your life? I have found that staying in the comfort zone is okay for a while, but it is rather boring.

Don't you want to live the best life you can ever live? Why settle for being less than you are when you can be so much more? Why are you intentionally restricting your existence on earth? Why are you happy to be where you are and not move up in life, to be a better parent, better worker, better wife, or better husband? You can take a risk and go back to school, be healthier, thinner, richer, and move higher on the ladder of life, if for no other reason than to reach down and help others up the ladder.

When you let your thoughts, feelings, and decisions be motivated by fear, you have already been reduced to being a slave of fear. I have come across people whose lives are very centered on the theme of fear, and it is a very disempowering state to be in. I have seen salespeople who are scared to make the phone call. They talk about someday owning their own business but will not take the first step to start the business. Their (mental) fears drive their thoughts, feelings, decisions, and behaviors so much that their life has become a by-product of fear, rather than their own desires. Mark had the potential to be a Navy diver, but fear was standing between him and the dream. If he let fear stop him, then he would have never achieved the dream to be a Navy diver, and this was the first step to achieving a bigger dream of becoming an Explosive Ordnance Disposal Technician.

Realize that there is a huge amount of potential packed in each and every one of us. When you let fear overcome you, you are letting fear mummify all that potential in you. To overcome fear is to move toward becoming a better you. It's all part of your growth journey.

3. Fear will follow you if you try to run away.

Not facing your fears is okay, and in many things we do in life we will never have to face the fear again. Many soldiers who come home and get out of the military will never have to go back into battle and face someone who is trying to kill them. You may turn down a chance to parachute, bungee jump, or climb a mountain, and in life the opportunity may not come again, so the wall of fear will never be in your path.

But if God has put a dream into your heart, or you have a strong desire to do something great with your life, it will seem that you keep facing the wall of fear over and over. Every time you face it you know you must go over it, around it, under it, or through it, and just like trying to run from your feet, you can never get away from them. Mark thought he could get away from the water and avoid the pool, but every time he turned around and wanted to do something great with his life in the Navy, it seemed that water was one of the common denominators for his dreams and success.

If you want to be number one in sales and you fear talking to people, then you will have to face the wall of fear over and over again. If you try to run from it, avoid it, spend as little time near it as possible, then you will struggle tremendously. It is only when you make the hard decision to go through the wall, to educate yourself, to learn new sales techniques, to speak better, to ask questions, and to learn to shut up when it is time to shut up—it is only then that you will blast through the wall and become good in sales.

Mark said to himself, "If I want this, I must do this," and that was when things started to change for him. He said to himself, "If I want to be a Navy diver, then I must swim confidently and not fear going underwater." That was the beginning step. From there he laid out a plan to hit the pool and become proficient and comfortable in the water. His plan included the following things:

- Exercising and becoming physically ready for Dive School
- Learning the content of the *U.S. Navy Diving Manual* by taking a correspondence course on it
- Talking with Navy divers and Explosive Ordnance Disposal Technicians about their jobs

It is when Mark stopped running away from the wall of fear, created a plan, and executed it that he was able to slowly break through the wall. So if you want your dream to come true or just to get past the fear, you will have to say, "If I want X, I will have to do Y." There will be some sacrifice that you will have to make. You have to pay a price for success. You have to pay a price to overcome your fears, too.

4. We never fully run away from fear.

When Mark decided to stay away from water, thinking that his problem was now solved, he made an error. He didn't know that when you run away from fear in one thing you will face another fear in another situation. The fear can be the same situation or field of business or totally different. Mark kept finding himself back at the pool because water is part of the Navy and Mark was also part of the Navy. As long as you let fear permeate you, as long as you run away from fear instead of dealing with it, it will always be there in your life, haunting you in everything you do. There is never an end point where you can successfully run away from fear, because it will always be there. Business owners tell me that they like the major part of the business but not all the things that come with it. They like fixing cars and enjoy the auto repair business, but many do not like dealing with the paperwork and employees who do not show up to work on time. They say they fear making bookkeeping errors and fear the IRS.

When you are young there are fears about finding a job, but as you get older there is a fear of having enough income for retirement. If you are fearful in job A, you can try to run away to job B—but you will face fear again in job B. You may think you are safe when you initially get a job, but you soon find out that the job may not be secure or may be a dead-end job, and you may not make enough money for retirement. So at some time in the future you will face the fear of retirement. So you really didn't escape fear. Running is temporary and not a good strategy for life.

The problem is your perception of reality and your inability to deal with fear. As long as you continue your current mode of thinking, you will always face fear in your life. You will never fully escape it. You can only try to keep running and running, but eventually you are going to find yourself backed into a corner, with no way out.

When that happens, you either have to learn to deal with it or to cower in its presence and become a fraction of the person you could be. If you chose to overcome your fear, you need to take action now, rather than waste all that time and energy avoiding it.

5. You pass on the fear to others.

When you hold on to fear, you accept it as your reality and run from it instead of facing it. As you do so, you may inadvertently teach others to also fear the same things you fear. I have seen people jump because they saw a snake and other people around them who did not see a snake also jump because the other person's fear reaction was picked up by them and they reacted. In war, when soldiers get scared and turn and run, others see the fear on their faces and that can cause others to get scared and start to run.

Mothers and fathers teach their children to avoid things that they feared themselves as a child. They may even teach them to run from things when there is no rational fear, just a perceived fear passed on to the children. Parents who have learned to face their fears will push their children and those they love to have courage and face the fears, to work hard and overcome them.

Mark was taught to "adapt, improvise, and overcome" when faced with a problem. How many times in school are children taught this lesson? Our teachers say no one should be left behind, but is that fair to the children who have faced their fear to write the report, do the research, and overcome the challenges only to see the lazy, the underachiever, be pulled up with them and allowed to get the reward without doing the work?

If there is a fear that the child will not pass, then the teacher's fear of telling the child or the parent that the child will not pass is not greater than the injustice done to the hardworking student and the student who didn't meet the grade. All of them—the failing child, the hardworking child, the teacher, and the parents—were cheated in the process. The hardworking student saw an unfair situation and may see his effort as a waste of time because the reward and grade is the same, even though the effort he put out was greater. The teacher didn't face her fear of giving a failing grade to the under-achieving student. The parents may have faced the fact that their child is not performing to standard, but feared the work needed to bring the child up to the school's standards to pass. And the student who didn't face the fear of hard work, doing the homework, and working hard for the grade is cheated, too, because at some time in his or her future an employer will not pull them along if they are not making a profit for the company. They will be left behind. Why do children that fail get passed along in school? Because the school fears losing funding because the students are not passing or the teachers may fear losing their jobs because the students are not passing the class. These fears are passed on from teacher to teacher, parents to parents, and from school system to school system. How many generations will have to be cheated until the fear is overcome and the school system faces the challenge of correcting this kind of situation?

We cannot pass our fears on to others when it comes to teaching. When Mark went to Navy schools, they said, "You will meet the grade and pass the tests and retests if needed, or you are dropped from training." Why would you lower the bar and pass students who do not meet the grade? Forcing students to perform is the right thing to do, but we cannot pass students who do not perform to a given standard. U.S. Navy divers are the best in the world only because the standards are high. Mark was expected to perform with or without his fear. If teachers, instructors, or trainers of any kind are afraid to fail students because of loss of funding, ridicule, or losing their jobs, then they are doing an injustice to the school system, students, and to themselves. When Mark was told he failed the Air Crewman swim test, was he hurt? Yes, he was, but he was not confident in the water and he did not meet the grade. That fact did not instill in him a quitter mentality, however. What it did do was make him determined to not fail another swim test. He worked harder in the pool so he would not fail. Why? Because he knew the feeling of failing a swim test and leaving the pool with his head down. Sometimes a failure will increase the resolve in a person.

Many parents shelter their children and pass their own fears to their children:

- "Don't climb a tree, because you may fall out."
- "Don't take a risk, because you may get hurt—be safe and stay at home."
- "Don't try out for that position, because you may be rejected."
- "Don't go camping, because you may get bitten by a mosquito and get malaria.
- "Don't compete in that event—what if you fail?"

We treat our children as if we think that all failure—the inability to pass a class or not getting a trophy—will crush their spirit. The reality is, however, that if they are determined to do something, a parent cannot stop them. If we live life to the fullest we will have pain, we will have to work hard, we will have problems, and we will make mistakes. We cannot blame others for the outcomes; we have to take responsibility for our life. When Columbus left Spain to find the new route to India, there were no guarantees, no tour guides or maps to follow, no hotels, no restaurants, no AAA or 911 emergency operator. When U.S. settlers headed West, they didn't go to MapQuest, but fear never stopped them from taking a calculated risk.

Life is risk—there are no guarantees—and why should you hold others responsible for your risk and for your not thinking there may be a consequence? If you drink hot coffee and get burned, the judge should tell you that you are an idiot, and unsafe, not give you money from a successful business owner (and pay the salary and nice home of a lawyer in the process). Now if you sold a kindergarten kid the hot coffee, there may be a case for the child's family, but not an adult coffee drinker of 30 years. You should know that if it is coffee, it is hot.

So now we have passed on to the new generation that taking the risk of owning a business is bad and that it is wise to be fearful of lawsuits. We teach them that there are predators waiting for a reason to get rich off of your success and hard work in business. We pass on that we should blame others for our mistakes and bad risks.

Many children are scared of terrorists but have never experienced a terrorist attack or have seen a terrorist except on TV. The fear has been passed on to us, so we don't fly, we don't go to crowded places, we are scared to live and scared to speak out in protest. We pass the fear on and allow it to become part of our lives instead of giving the fear back to those who try to force fear onto us.

If the fear of what happens to a terrorist when caught is greater than the fear of doing the terrorist act, then the terrorist will not commit the act. But if you get three meals a day, room and board, free DVD movies, library privileges, and free lawyers, then the terrorist will see this as a real good deal (no fear for them).

We must stop passing the fear on to others, we must learn to face our fears and live life with the risk of failure, we must live up to our potential and challenge ourselves, our children, and those we come in contact with during our lives. We must face our fears and take risks with courage or stay home and quit blaming others.

America was made great because we have had people who were not afraid to face their fears. As it is said in the last line of the Declaration of Independence, "… we mutually pledge to each other our Lives, our Fortunes and our sacred Honor." We must face our fears and take risks with courage or stay home and quit blaming others.

America's founders did not pass on fear to us! They faced the wall of fear and were willing to lose their lives, their fortunes, and their sacred honor. How many of us are willing to give it all up for our cause? Do we even tell our children that we are ready to face fear for them, for our morals and values, and to give our life for our country? Or to give our life for our family members?

6. When you overcome one fear, you grow in the process, and this helps you overcome other fears.

When Mark faced his fears and made the decision to try out to become a Navy diver, he had no idea that he could do it. But the decision to do it was made first. Many people say that when they know how to do a business, they will start it, or when they know how to swim well, they will be a diver. Or when they can speak well, they will run for elected office. Well, if you are waiting for the knowledge, then you will never do it, you will never risk anything, and you will never face your fears. We learn in the process of doing and by doing.

Mark made the decision first and then asked, "How do I do it?" People start a business and learn as they go. Columbus set sail for the New World but did not have a map to get there. He drew the map as he went. The decision to go always comes first. When Columbus came back to Spain, he wanted to go to the New World again and again, because he grew in courage and knowledge by taking the first risk and building on that. John F. Kennedy made the decision to go to the Moon before the decade was out, but did not know how we would do that. The decision always comes first. From that decision there was a lot of risk taking, a lot of fears to break through, and many learning experiences. From that decision, other countries have gained the courage to also go into space.

When we say we are scared and do not move forward and face our fears we start a pattern of seeing situations that are risky as a reason for not moving forward. However, if we move toward the wall of fear and break through it, when we are faced with another wall we will say that it is possible to go through that wall also, and we will create the pattern that walls are not dead ends, only challenges to conquer. The bend in the road is not the end of the road unless we fail to make the turn.

7. Fear is all in our mind.

Fear of the unknown, fear of the future, fear of terrorism, fear of clowns, and fear of the dark are fears that are in our mind without any rational basis. Mental fear is based on a danger made up in your mind. This fear arises because your brain somehow formulated a perception that these non-physical dangers are real dangers—when they are not.

Some people will point out that it's not from the physical harm where people get fear—but from the thought of slipping up, people judging you, the embarrassment that will occur, and what may happen or could happen. These fears are all in your mind. You have thought of these things and have created fear when other people have thought of these same things and did not get scared.

Even if something has happened in the past, it does not mean that the same thing is going to happen in the future. You are in the present and not the future. You are still in a position to control your thinking, but if you let fear get a hold on you, then you have given control to the fear and have already lost the battle.

Mark feared the water but saw other people who loved the water, so all he had to do was to change his thinking from fear to love and it would change his future—and it did.

8. Fear is a waste of our energy.

Mental fear is highly illogical and a waste of emotional and mental energy. When we fear something we need to look at the situation and ask: "What is it that we fear? Is it real? Can we get injured or killed? What steps do we need to take to protect ourselves? Should we avoid this?" Then we need to move *toward* the fear with courage. After that decision is made, then fear and worry is a waste of time and energy.

After making a rational decision, whenever you spend one moment being fearful and thinking about what you fear, you are wasting your time and energy on something that does not propel you forward. Every moment you spend thinking something negative and fearful is just like planting a seed in a garden that grows and gives rises to subsequent similar thoughts. The more you do it, the more you are set back by it. Instead of calmly processing the situation and rationally identifying solutions and ways forward, you are feeding energy into something that isn't constructive.

Fear leads to a rush of adrenaline that gives you increased physical performance, not increased mental performance. You are now excited and ready to run or fight, but there is nothing threatening you. You can think about solutions just as well, if not better, without all the adrenaline that's pumping through your body. So calm down—having more adrenaline in your body for prolonged periods of time strains your body and gives you jittery nerves instead.

Remember that for every moment you spend being fearful, you have one less moment for positive thoughts and feelings. So control your fears and use your energy to break through the wall of fear and stop wasting your time and energy worrying about what might happen.

Mark had a Commanding Officer who taught him a very valuable lesson that he carries through life. At a conference meeting, a Chief brought a problem to the meeting. The Commanding Officer said, "What are we going to do about it?" The Chief said, "I don't know, that is why I am telling you." The Commanding Officer said, "Don't bring me your problems without researching possible solutions first. When you bring up a problem I want three solutions, and I will pick the best one. I do not have all the answers, and I do not know your situation in your department as well as you do."

Why should the Commanding Officer spend time on your problems? You know yourself better than anyone else does. So work on solutions and plans to overcome your problems and your fears. Research the fearful situation, get advice, education, and then take action.

We must look for solutions to every fear, every risk, and every problem. New inventions are developed because someone would not accept things as they are. They took the risk of developing something to make life better and easier, and for the possibility of reward in the form of wealth for themselves and their family.

So Mark learned to not only identify problems but to find multiple solutions for them.

CHAPTER 15

FEAR IS THE DRIVING
COMPONENT!

Most of you reading this book will agree with me that when you were a child you had dreams for your future, what you would do when you grew up and what job you would have. As children we did not see obstacles—we didn't rationally think about how we would do it, where the money would come from, who would help us achieve our goals (lawyer, bookkeeper, accountant, and so on), the education we would need to make our dreams come true, and most of all, we didn't even think of fear as a component that might stop us on our journey.

Why is it that adults (grandparents, uncles, and aunts) have always asked children this question: "What do you want to be when you grow up?"? Is it because they want to know the child's plans? Are they looking for a partner for their business? Is it to see the wild dreams the child's mind can come up with? No—I think it is because children have no fear of failure and dream BIG. And this is exciting! How many of us lost our dream, changed our dream or have given up on our dream? Most older people will encourage the young children and tell them to take a risk.

I think that adults are looking to regain the thinking they had when they were children. Children have the ability to dream, without having a plan and without letting fear get in the way. I believe that fear is a big component in stopping people from achieving their dreams, pursuing their dreams, and dreaming *very big dreams.*

If there were no fear of failure, what would you do with your life? Would you try harder, risk more, never quit until you succeed? Would you invest more money and help more people? Would you go on more vacations, hike in the woods, go for walks at night? Would you really live life more adventurously?

Children have not been taught to fear failure, to fear risking money, the fear of embarrassment in a venture, or even to fear doing something stupid. It seems that as they get older they run into "loving" people who have fears and pass them on in "loving" ways that instill fear into them. What do I mean?

How many people in your life have said words to the effect of:

- "Who do you think you are to do that?"
- "Where are you going to get the money?"
- "Where are you going to get the education to do that?"
- "What makes you think you can succeed when others have failed?"
- "You're not smart enough to do that—maybe your brother or sister could, but not you!"
- "I don't think you have what it takes to do that."

These things are never told to children when they say, "I want to be a policeman, an astronaut, a dancer, the president when I grow up."

But once you are older there seems to be people in your life who put roadblocks out on the path to your dreams—they let you know of all the things that could go wrong with your plans and ideas. They tell you stories of people who tried what you want to do and failed. They ask you questions that you don't want to hear, such as, "Who's going to pay for your education? I'm only telling you this because I don't want you to get hurt."

They slowly chip away at your dream; they ask you questions that make you believe that you are not ready to live out your dream, start the business, or began the journey. These people are bullies, dream stealers;

they are the people on the ladder of life who are holding your legs and telling you that it is scary up at the top. They try to hold you back, "for your own good." They don't want to see you get hurt, lose money, or be a failure. They are "loving." The truth is that they have never been to the top, and they surely don't want you to try to go to the top. You will be much better off if you get away from these people and do not listen to their advice, because these are the bullies who are putting roadblocks in your path.

Mark was very lucky because he decided to do something great with his life. He did not know what that would be or how he was going to do it, but there was an inner drive, something pulling at him to have more, do more, and become more, and he was not ignoring this feeling. He never told anyone in the Navy, or his family, that he had this dream. There was no one to tell him he could not do it or pursue it. He did not have a bully in his life who was putting roadblocks in his path. So when Mark decided to try out for Navy diver—and ultimately EOD— he met little resistance. As a matter of fact, the Navy divers and EOD were always recruiting new people (because it is a voluntary position in the Navy) and they spoke positively about the program and were very encouraging. They did not know Mark was scared of the water and that he was not in great physical shape for their elite program. They just told him to swim, run, and physically train as often as possible. They said, in effect, "You can do it."

If you talk to people who have been successful in any field in life, they will always encourage you to try. They know it will be hard; nothing of great value in life comes easily. But successful people never see things as roadblocks—only hurdles to get over, go around, or to go through. They are usually the people who will help you plan, get the education, or show you some of the challenges you will have to overcome.

Most of all, these people who believe in your dream will paint a picture of what a day will be like once you achieve your dream. They will encourage you to succeed, and they will tell you what it will be like when you get there. Mark was told by the EOD guys that he will dive all over the nation and the world, he will do demolition on land and underwater, he will drive boats, four-wheel drive trucks, he will learn to parachute, he will be in the best physical shape of his life, and he will use and train with equipment valued in the thousands to millions of dollars. He will do things that James Bond did in the movies, will put on ordnance demonstrations, train with guns, and will help save the lives of soldiers, sailors, and civilians. Of course, it will be dangerous work, but the Navy will train you to be a professional, he was told.

So the reality is that no one is ready with everything in place when they start to plan something new in their life. There will always be the unknown things you forgot to plan for, the events that just happen on the way, and challenges to overcome. But get away from the people who love you too much and try to steal your dream. Look for the people who have done what you want to do and tell them what you want to do—they will give you the truth and will most likely encourage you on your way.

Fear will either stop you in your tracks on the path, or fear and the dream will cause you to prepare, plan, and push forward.

Mark was scared of the water, and the voice of fear could have told him, "Who do you think you are? You can't swim, you can only do the dog paddle and breaststroke a short distance, you're afraid to put your head in the water, and you are not in great physical shape like these guys. You'll never make it."

However, the voice of courage said, "Give it a try, create a physical training plan, get in the pool at lunchtime, read all you can, and ask questions of the Navy divers and EOD."

Mark would not let fear become an option—he focused on the results and that was to graduate Dive School.

Fear is the driving component to either move you forward or to stop you in your tracks, turn you around, and to make you run away. It is either fight or flight. Mark chose to fight, and he did not let "quit," "can't," or "give up" become part of his vocabulary. As a matter of fact, Mark actually went home, got a pen with black ink, and crossed out "can't" in the dictionary.

Years later, when his children said they couldn't do something, he told them "can't" is not a word, and when they argued, he told them it is not in the dictionary. When they looked it up they said someone crossed it out and he said, "See, I told you it is not in the dictionary."

"Can't" was not an option and not a word in his vocabulary, he did not allow roadblocks, even in his self-talk.

CHAPTER 16

ACCEPT FEAR AND MOVE ON?

I t is sad that there are people who fear things that they shouldn't, and that there are those that do not fear things that they should. Many of us have gotten ourselves into certain situations that when we look back make us say, "I shouldn't have done that. I should have thought before I did that. I ignored the voice inside that said not to do it." We also see the little child who has no fear to stop him or her from walking into the street, stepping off the top stair, or reaching for the hot pot on the stove.

What is the most disturbing is to see people who accept fear as part of their life. They are so fearful that they actually allow the pressure to hold them back from enjoying life. They will not go to Hawaii because they fear flying, they will not go to Disney World because they fear driving long distances, they do not go to Las Vegas because they fear sleeping in a strange bed, and they do not visit relatives or go to family reunions because they fear being around groups of people. The joys of life are covered by layers of fear—the fears of getting old, getting sick, losing money, rejection, failure, losing a job, moving to a better city and lifestyle. Some people are afraid of dying, but the fear doesn't prevent them from dying, it only prevents them from living!

If fear is not conquered and controlled, it has the ability to mutate and grow. It can cause aggression, anger, hopelessness, worry, high blood pressure, suspicion, anxiety, and many other negative emotions. How sad it would be to die and have never had the chance to become the person we were meant to be and do the things we were meant to do in life!

Fear, when based on rational thought, can be a warning that will protect us. When fear is based on wild imaginings and false beliefs, then it is like a ball and chain that has a negative effect on our life experiences. It may even bring on other emotions that further increase the negative side of life. Many political liberals let fear hold them back from living life and making good laws that develop people and do not make them dependent. They blame others because of their fears and pass laws to ensure they are guaranteed money, wealth, and an easy life where they do not have to risk anything. How foolish it would have been if Mark had thought this way!

If Mark let the fear of water hold him back from living a more exciting life, expanding his knowledge of diving, underwater life, and helping the U.S. Navy, where would he be today? By conquering the fear, he changed negative emotions and events into something else. He turned them (through hard work) into positive emotions, and by doing so enjoyed an increase in confidence and self-worth, an expansion of his knowledge, and a participation in the new worlds of travel, underwater life, and enjoyment of the sea—and he was in the best physical shape of his life, too.

Your imagination draws to it whatever you are anticipating, just like a magnet draws metallic objects to it. If you expect the water to harm you, then it will; if you expect the water to be your friend, then it will be your friend; if you expect the water to be neutral, then it will be neutral.

If you expect the darkness to hold monsters, boogie men, and dangerous things, then the darkness will, but if you see the darkness as neutral, then it shall be neutral.

The anticipation of a test can be more fearful than the test itself; the anticipation of pain from a shot is more painful than the shot itself, which lasts a couple seconds.

Every anticipated fear has a great deal of emotion attached to it—anger, agitation, nervousness, heightened senses, racing heartbeat, high-pitched voice. We can easily become an emotional wreck with the onslaught of such emotions. To stop this from happening, you must *be aware* that you are becoming emotional when you are scared, you must *be aware* that there is a change in your body, and you must *consciously control* the emotion by means of your thoughts.

When you are fearful and aware of this fear, then you must take control of your thoughts before they take control of you. You must look at the thing you fear and ask yourself if there is danger in this thing. If there is danger in it, you must prepare for the worst that could happen. In most cases it is our imagination that creates far more danger than is real. Face that which you fear and say, "I am not afraid of you. I decide what I fear and when I have courage. And I choose courage. Fear, you are my friend and have kept me safe from harm in my life, but you will not stop me from living up to my full potential and enjoying new challenges."

"You gain strength, courage, and confidence by every experience in which you really stop to look fear in the face. You must do the thing which you think you cannot do."
– Eleanor Roosevelt

Many times in life we say, "I don't want to go to the party," just to hide that we are afraid to be in crowds of people. We may say, "Technology does not interest me," but in reality, we are afraid of new things. We may say when asked for our opinion, "I have nothing to add," but really we are afraid to speak in a group of people. Our greatest problem is not in what might happen. Our greatest problem is our fears. A small obstacle may stop the timid person from moving forward. But to the courageous person, the obstacle is only a challenge to get past.

"The only thing we have to fear Is fear itself." – Franklin D. Roosevelt

Mark was scared of the water, but it was not in running from the water or in fearing to act that he overcame his fear. Mark knew that if he was going to overcome the fear he would have to take action and get into the water—he would have to face the fear, and so he started taking baby steps.

"One of the greatest discoveries a man makes, one of his great surprises, is to find he can do what he was afraid he couldn't do." – Henry Ford

Discovering the joy of life can be as simple as being willing to accept discomfort. Can you get out of your comfort zone to face your fears, to tackle the giants and bullies that are holding you back? When you feel fear, can you say to yourself, "Get used to being uncomfortable"? If you cannot, you may just stay where you are in life.

But if you are not where you want to be in life, and it is not acceptable to you to stay where you are, then you must get on your feet, get uncomfortable, face the fear, and turn the obstacles into challenges to overcome.

Mark was uncomfortable in the water, Mark had fears of drowning, Mark had fears of failure, and Mark had the fear of failing the physical training test and losing face with his peers. But he knew where he was at in his life was unacceptable, because he had a bigger dream. He wanted to make more money for his growing family. He had to get out of his comfort zone, and get into the pool. He was extremely uncomfortable for over a year of his life until he got into the Dive School. But it did not stop there; he was uncomfortable in Dive School, in the pool, and on the grinder doing physical training. His muscles ached at night from the workout. But he knew these obstacles were challenges that he had to overcome. If you have a little fear, then you will have a little effort to put out to overcome it. But if the fear is great, then you will have to put out greater effort to overcome it.

"He who would accomplish little must sacrifice little; he who would achieve much must sacrifice much; he who would attain highly must sacrifice greatly." – James Allen

---

Many people think that Mark made the decision one time and that was enough to carry him through until the end. This is a fallacy. Anyone with a big dream—especially if the dream will take two years to complete, like it did for Mark—will need a big commitment. You will have to make the decision over and over many times during a week.

What does that mean?

It means that when you put your hand to the plow you don't look back until you have completed the job.

It means you never, *never* quit. It means your word is good, and you don't change your mind just because the situation no longer *feels* good. Once you are committed, feelings don't count. Emotions are pushed out of the way. It will not only not feel right, a lot of the time, but it will downright hurt a bunch. That is part of the process of taking anything of value to its completion. There is no gain without emotional and physical pain.

"Pain is weakness leaving the body."
– Navy Diving Instructors

Quitting was not an option, and the word "can't" was not in Mark's vocabulary. He had to get up every day and recommit to the dream, to the plan, and to the goal. Fear was not an option on the path to success.

Mark asked himself, "What did I get myself into? Why don't you just quit? What are you trying to prove?" But every time he asked himself those questions, he felt the pull on his heart telling him that he must do this. So quitting was not a conversation that he would allow. He would then recommit to completing what he set out to do.

Mark commented on commitment and said: "Once you go over the side of the boat, you are committed—no quitting, the air (tank) is on your back, you cannot say 'I quit,' you cannot take the regulator (mouthpiece) out, and breathing on your own is impossible." Once Mark decided to go to Dive School, he decided to pass. He was never dropped from training or from military schools, and he was now spending taxpayers' money and he would not quit. Since Dive School is voluntary, you have to request to quit training; however, the instructors can drop you from training for academics, physical deficiency, or for safety reasons. Mark said, "I will not quit voluntarily." The instructors would have to drop him for their own reasons.

If you intend to complete what you decide to do, you must be committed and have the continual self-talk that keeps you committed until the end. Fear is present for any endeavor of any great value. If there is no great value to overcome, then there is no challenge and thus there is no great fear.

Without fear there is no expansion of the comfort zone, and you limit your life and your future. Having fear and having pain is normal for all humans. Those who are afraid of fear also fear growth. And those who remove fear from the lives of others in the hope of protecting them also remove the opportunity for growth and expansion of others' comfort zones.

Face the fear, study the risks and the alternatives, be safe, and move forward with the fear, in spite of the fear.

"Fear makes come true that which one is afraid of." – Victor Frankl

The reality is that nothing in life of any value happens without fear. I think women can understand this because having a baby has to be scary and would require pain. However, many women accept the pain and fear but still move forward and have the baby.

A Congressional Medal of Honor recipient was being interviewed recently, and he was asked, "This may sound stupid, but ... were you afraid?" He said, "Yes, I was afraid!"

"So why did you get the Medal of Honor and your fellow men did not?" the interviewer asked.

He said, "They ran away from what they feared, and I ran toward it."

Life is out there to be conquered. But we will never do anything great if we follow the crowd, if we do as others want, if we run from that which we fear. When everyone is running backward, you move forward; when everyone is going right, you go left. When everyone fears the economy, you move toward the economic challenge. This is the way to stand out in the crowd, get recognized, and get past your fears and live life to the fullest.

Is Fear Real?

Fear is a feeling, and you make it real by your thoughts; you have the power to control it or let it control you.

"A man has to learn that he cannot command things, but that he can command himself; that he cannot coerce the wills of others, but that he can mold and master his own will: and things serve him who serves Truth; people seek guidance of him who is master of himself." – James Allen

As a child, Mark let the fear control him, and no one could change that, only Mark. In time and with experience he learned to control the fear and to control his thoughts. Mark knew that if you know what someone knows, and you do what someone does, then you can have what they have. Mark saw a man in the pool swim like a fish, and he knew his body was the same as that guy's, so if he copied the strokes, he should swim just like that guy.

"All that you accomplish or fail to accomplish with your life is the direct result of your thoughts." – James Allen

---

"Whether you be man or woman you will never do anything in this world without courage. It is the greatest quality of the mind next to honor." – James Allen

---

Fear can hold us back from doing the things we really love to do in life. Many times we want to help others, volunteer our time, and to pursue a life of service.

That is why when we see someone going beyond fear to show love to others we hold them in high regard. Mother Teresa helped many people in her life, and it was her devotion and great love of the human person that moved her to go beyond the fear of ridicule. She had to move beyond the fear of getting sick by helping the sick, the fear of becoming poor by giving her money to the poor, the fear of not having food for herself because she gave her food to the hungry, and the fear of being lowly by helping those that have been labeled by society as the lowly, sick, and destitute.

Self-preservation or self-love will persuade us to do things in life that may be selfish and prideful, or that may, we think, help us to save face. These attitudes may even stop us from doing things. For example, in Mark's case as a child, his fear was telling him there was danger, so it froze him in his tracks. Instead of trying to swim, he wanted to run away, and instead of listening to the instructors and doing as they said, he reached for the safety of the side of the pool.

Fear can hold us back because we want to survive, and the fear is telling us that there is a danger of death or injury. Only when we have enough love (for the dream, goal, or plan) and education to overcome the self-preservation thinking can we fight for what we want to do. We have all heard of the soldier in battle who thought more about saving a buddy's life. His love became a driving force, so he ignored the fears of his own death or injury to save his buddy. Similarly, a parent will risk his or her life to save their child who has stepped in front of a moving car.

On the other hand, we have also heard of the person who is frozen with fear and will watch someone get robbed or killed and will not even step forward to help. When we do not show love, it is because we have fear that is greater than the love inside of us. The fear becomes what we think about, and this fear overcomes the desire to love, the desire to show love, and the desire to get involved.

Many marriages and friendships break apart because of fear, the fear of losing face, the fear of embarrassment, the fear of peer pressure, fear of not belonging, the fear of loss of love, the fear of being poor, the fear of life getting worse, the fear of taking care of a sickly spouse or parent, the fear of the partner getting old, wrinkly, saggy, and bald.

If we all followed in the footsteps of Mother Teresa and let love be our guiding force, old folks and nursing homes would soon disappear and go out of business. Divorce would decrease, families would be closer, and the sick, homeless, and hungry would decrease and may even disappear in our lifetime.

Many organizations advertise that they want to end hunger, shelter the homeless, and find cures for the sick. But if they will not promote good morals for our society, stand up for the rights of the unborn and elderly, or allow good morals, respect, and love of family and love of country in our schools and public places, or even on our personal property and in our family life, then they're like the person who throws logs on the fire to smother it. They are only feeding the fire in the name of doing good.

The love they want in our world that will ultimately end in peace (the peace that they are protesting for) will only come when the love starts in their hearts and souls. Then it will radiate to the words and actions of people, to society, to the country, and then to other nations and the whole world.

Mark could not promote thoughts of swimming success while promoting fear of the water in his mind, heart, and soul. Elected government officials cannot promote peace, love, and care for the people's needs when they promote selfishness (in their wealth building and owning of cars and homes, and in their lavish lifestyles), take bribes, money from the taxpayers, and lie to the people in their campaigns for election.

Whenever we see a person who truly loves others, they deny themselves something in the process. Love overcomes their fears. On the other hand, when we see people with fear, it is because they are selfish and are thinking of their own self-preservation and do not have a strong enough love to propel them past the fear.

We have seen throughout history many politicians and presidents who have put their love of country and love of people first, and their policies and actions followed the love that was in their minds, hearts, and souls. They went down in history as good presidents and politicians. On the other hand, we have seen very selfish, ruthless, lying, and backbiting by those who have fear in their minds, hearts, and souls. Their lack of love for their country, and for other people appears for all to see in their words and actions.

Mark's love of his country and his devotion to job and family came out for all to see in his overcoming his fears and moving forward to be the best sailor he could be.

CHAPTER 17

GOD'S VIEWPOINT ON FEAR AND OVERCOMING IT

Fear does not make a thing right or wrong. Fear is a component of life. You can be doing everything right in your life and feel fear. Like a soldier in battle who is obeying all orders and is doing his job, one can be in the right place doing the right things but still be scared.

How do God's people deal with fear?

A thief in the night is doing the wrong things but is also scared of getting caught. Fear does not make a thing right or wrong. Fear may be a warning to be cautious, or a reminder that you need to move faster or slower or you need to think about how you act or present yourself in a new situation.

"Fear opens our eyes to the Lord."
– 2 Kings 19:14-19

Fear is not an indicator that you are doing the wrong things. Many times in life you can be on the right path, pursuing your dreams, but are scared to death. You can be opening a new business, writing a book, or going back to school and you feel your stomach churning. The little voice inside says, "What are you doing? Who do you think you are? Do you really believe this is the path to success?" Doubt and fear seem to go hand in hand.

Do not think that because there is fear that you are doing the wrong thing. Fear is telling you that you are in an unfamiliar land and that you need to be cautious and look out for danger. This is a normal reaction, but many people in life think that if it was the right thing, the right dream, and the right time, everything would fall into place. So they come to the conclusion that this must be the wrong time, the wrong dream, and the wrong thing to do.

Throughout the Bible are examples of heroes who were scared but pressed forward and did the right things, becoming heroes of the Bible. David fought a giant Philistine named Goliath—do you think he was not scared? When Moses had to go tell Pharaoh to let the Israelites go he was scared and even said to God that he was not a good speaker, and God said he would send Aaron with him to help. Noah was ridiculed for building a boat on dry land. Yet they all continued in the face of danger, ridicule, fear, and rejection. Fear is a component that needs to be rationally thought about, contemplated, and planned for. Many people in life dream of business success, a best-selling book, a career change, and so on, but in their planning leave out the component of fear and how to deal with it. They often also leave out the component of the "Border Bullies" who tell you that you do not have what it takes to succeed, that you do not have the knowledge, or the money, or the patience to succeed.

We never plan for fear to happen, and these "Border Bullies" can unknowingly steal the dream from us. For example, a mother tries to keep her children from being hurt, disappointed, or feeling rejection, so she tells them that going into business is not a good idea, that they don't have what it takes, that going off to college and away from home is risky, and that it is okay to live at home. So, even though she has good intentions, she is really a "Border Bully," because we know she should say, "Go ahead and try it, because you will learn many things and become a stronger person in the process."

We must put the component of fear into our plans. We must think about questions like these:

- "How do I deal with fear?"
- "Is this fear real?"
- "How much fear will I feel when it happens?"
- "How will I deal with it when it does happen, which it will?"

Many people would rather die than to speak in front of a group of people. This fear is usually based on some previous experience that may have not been good, such as when a music teacher tells a student to get in front of the class and sing a song to the class. Once the child's voice cracks and the other students laugh, thoughts of never getting into a situation like that again run through the child's mind. This may be fine if you have done this before and if you have a stellar voice. But for the everyday child who doesn't even sing at home with his family, this kind of experience can be devastating, and he or she may never want to get in front of a group of people again.

Whenever they are confronted with a similar situation the thoughts and flashbacks to the embarrassing and painful event will have fear running up and down their spines. Again, it is normal to have flashbacks; but it is how a person deals with this situation that will determine if they move forward or backward. Some people say that self-talk is a way to get through a situation that causes fear, but only if it is positive and you ignore the fear and move forward. But whatever you decide to do, the fear is still there to prevent you from doing something foolish or careless. Self-preservation always remains as the primary motivator in unknown or uncharted territory.

The reality is that not all people will be able to go past their fears and that all people will not attain a level of proficiency in an atmosphere of high stress and intense problem solving.

There is fear that can grab you, hold you tight, and occupy so much of your rational thinking that you will be frozen with terror, and in such cases you will not act even to save your own life. Some people have *not* been taught how to react in a given situation and they freeze up because of fear. For example, take a bank robbery. Many times there are more people than gunmen, but the fear of getting shot or the fear of death freezes everyone—when they could have overpowered the gunman. When you do not react it is because the fear has a hold on you and you are letting the fear control you.

Being so terrified that one freezes and cannot act is a rare circumstance but nonetheless something that *can* happen—a reality—especially when you are faced with an event that you have never experienced before.

In the case of Mark, as a child he was so scared that he did not learn to swim well enough to pass the Boy Scouts first class swim test, even after two classes. However, with age and experience, the fear was conquered over time. He fully experienced the fear, and he broke it into smaller pieces. Doing that allowed him to slowly gain confidence. He swam for longer periods of time, gained knowledge about how to be proficient in the various swimming strokes, gained physical strength, and gained the confidence to continue to overcome fear, wherever he experienced it.

How did Mark overcome his fear? God had placed the dream in his heart and soul, and he had blessed him with the ability to persevere in the face of fear.

"Do not let your hearts be troubled or afraid." – John 14:27

Mark overcame his fear by doing five basic things:

1. He *nurtured* his strong **desire and determination** to be a Navy diver and EOD.
2. He *dedicated* himself to becoming the best **professional** sailor he could be and to do his duty for his country.

3. He *disciplined* himself, set up a **plan**, and worked the plan.
4. He *worked* on his **attitude**.
5. He *decided* from the beginning to **never quit**.

"Behold, I am instructing you. Be strengthened, and be steadfast. Do not dread, and do not fear. For the Lord your God is with you in all things, wherever you may go." – Joshua 1:9

By the grace of God, good things happened to Mark. Fear had a hold on him, though; many times he tried to overcome the fear of the water but was unsuccessful. So, Mark prayed for success in life. He didn't know what the success would look like or where it would come from. He never knew what road to take. Would it be in business, working hard on a job? He knew if he prayed and let God's will guide him, that God would open doors for him and guide him on the right path. Many people pray for something, expecting it to happen as they want and not listening to God's will. As God answered Mark's prayers, he was patient enough to let things unfold as God wanted. If Mark listened to his fear and got his way, success would have never been in the water. Mark knew that God's path was always the right path, no matter how hard it might be.

God opened doors for mark in his life that were impossible for him to open by himself. As stated in Revelation 3:8 I know thy works (behold, I have set before thee a door opened, which none can shut), that thou hast a little power, and didst keep my word, and didst not deny my name. (American Standard Version)

"The Lord foils the plan of nations, frustrates the designs of peoples. But the plan of the Lord stands forever, wise designs through all generations." – Psalms 33:10

Mark was inspired by his Senior Chief to get healthy, not to get in the water. He went to the gym, and people and events kept pushing him in the direction that God wanted. Navy divers recruited him and encouraged him. The bomb scare in the building he worked at sent EOD to the site, and curiosity inspired Mark to go talk with the EOD personnel. The career counselor who told him he was getting near the cut-off age for diver, EOD, and SEALs said he would have to apply now or forget them. All these things pushed him in a direction that was really pushing against his fear. But God does not know fear! Humans know fear, but God does not. God is love, and where there is love there is no fear.

That is why some think that if Jesus is God, how could he experience fear? Since Jesus is God and Man, Divine and Human, he experienced all the human emotions—and he did experience fear. In Matthew 26:38, Jesus said to Peter and the two sons of Zebedee, "My soul is sorrowful even to Death. Remain here and keep watch with me." Then he fell prostrate in prayer and said, "My Father, if it is possible, let this cup pass from me; yet, not as I will, but as you will." Jesus felt fear and knew his future suffering, and he pleaded for a different way. Jesus did what we should do with our fear, and that is to pray to God.

The best response to fear is to pray to God. Psalm 56:4 says, "When I am afraid, in you I place my trust."

Our fears should lead us to God; he should be our source of strength, courage, and protection. Don't feel bad and put yourself down for feeling fear. Just place your fears in the loving arms of God.

The Bible mentions two types of fear. The first type is beneficial and is to be encouraged. The second type is a detriment and is to be overcome. The first type of fear is "fear of the Lord." This type of fear is the awe of God, a reverence for His power and glory. It is also a proper respect for his wrath and anger. Fear of the Lord brings with it many blessings and benefits.

Psalm 111:10 says, "The fear of the Lord is the beginning of wisdom; all those who practice it have a good understanding. His praise endures forever!" This fear is a good fear that helps us to grow in reverence and wisdom.

The second type of fear mentioned in the Bible is not good at all, and we should learn to overcome these fears. This is the "spirit of fear" mentioned in 2 Timothy 1:7: "For God has not given us a spirit of fear, but of power and of love and of a sound mind" (NKJV). Fear does not come from God, and fearfulness and timidity is not from God. Beginning in the book of Genesis and continuing throughout the book of Revelation, God reminds us to "fear not."

Isaiah 41:10 says, "Do not fear, for I am with you; Do not anxiously look about you, for I am your God. I will strengthen you, surely I will help you, Surely I will uphold you with My righteous right hand."

In Psalm 56:11, the psalmist writes, "In God I trust; I will not be afraid. What can man do to me?" This is an awesome testimony to the power of trusting in God. The key to overcoming fear is total and complete trust in God. Trusting God is a decision not to give in to fear. It is a turning to God even in the darkest times and trusting Him to make things right. This trust comes from knowing God and knowing that He is good. Once we have learned to put our trust in God, we will no longer be afraid of the things that come against us.

"The wise man in the storm prays God, not for safety from danger, but for deliverance from fear." – Ralph Waldo Emerson

---

Take time to listen to your emotions. Fear, anger, depression, disappointment, frustration, loneliness, and sorrow are classified as negative emotions, but that does not make them "wrong." It is what we do in response to our emotions that make them good or bad. In fact positive and negative emotions are morally neutral. Negative emotions should awaken us to take positive action and constructive action. Emotions pull at us to engage our mind and to make wise decisions on our course of action. We should pray to the Holy Spirit for wisdom, because we do not have as much knowledge as God. When we make wise decisions and good plans, emotions have served their purpose.

"I sought the LORD, who answered me,
delivered me from all my fears."
– Psalms 34:5

Norman Vincent Peale, the minister-author who taught a generation about positive thinking, gives the following ten ways to overcome your fear in his "Help yourself with God's help" pamphlet, *How to get rid of Fear*:

1. **Seek** – Seek God's help.
2. **Trust** – Trust in God.
3. **Rely** – Rely on God.
4. **Study** – Study the basis of your fear.
5. **Add** – Add what your past successes were, build on this.
6. **Do** – Do the thing you fear.
7. **Courage** – Have courage to face fear.
8. **See** – See yourself doing the thing you fear.
9. **Help** – Help others get over their fear.
10. **Faith** – Believe in God's help and in yourself.

"There is no fear in Love, but perfect love drives out fear because fear
has to do with punishment, so one who fears is not yet
perfect in Love." – 1 John 4:18

Some experiences you might have as God helps you with your fears:

1. Belief in God's help comes as you pray for help and as you succeed.
2. You must be patient to see how God will get you through.
3. When God tests you, you must trust in God.

4. When you get past the wall of fear, you become stronger—it is God refining you, like gold being tried in a fire.

5. God tests us in the area of our greatest weakness, for example, patience, anger, and fear.

6. How does your attitude fare in time of fear? With God's help you stay positive and strong.

7. God will open and close doors in your life as he sees fit, so sometimes you will not be able to move in the direction that you think—be flexible and pray for guidance.

8. When under pressure, the "true you" comes out. When you squeeze an orange what comes out? Answer: Orange juice. So when you are under pressure what is inside comes out (anger, patience, quitter attitude, and so on).

CHAPTER 18

FEAR OF PUBLIC SPEAKING

W hy are so many people scared of public speaking? Many people have said that they would rather die than give a public speech. There may be many reasons why they feel this way. It could be:

- They are speaking on a subject they have no interest and no passion about.
- They were pressured in school to give a speech, and they failed.
- They were not taught how to outline a speech, how to stand, how to present, and have a lack of public-speaking skills.
- As an audience member, the person was never taught to respect the speaker and tended to ridicule instead of praise the efforts of others who attempted to deliver a speech.
- Many people told them they will never be a good speaker because they are shy, and they received no encouragement.
- They may say the wrong things to themselves, such as, "I am not good at this" and other negative self-talk.

Good speakers are not born with the gift, but are made through speaking, learning, and practice.

It may also be that they are asking themselves questions to justify quitting, such as:

- "Why do I want to give a public speech?"
- "Why should I do this at all?"
- "Why is this important?"
- "What can I possibly learn this?"
- "Will the audience laugh at me?
- "I do not have the talent for this, who do I think I am?"

When a person has a dream to run for public office, or a desire to be a teacher, preacher, or even a salesman, they know they will have to speak to people or in front of people, and some of these people will be high-ranking people in the community. In this case, their passion and dream will overpower their fear, and they will persist, learn, and practice to be proficient in speaking. Only when their passion is greater than their fear will they seek the tools and education they need to pull this off.

There are many self-help books written on how to overcome the fear of public speaking. Most people will *not* read them because they do not have the desire to speak in public. However, once there is a dream, desire, or the push from the right loving people, they will seek these books and practice to become the best public speaker they can be. Is it easy? No! It will be a journey of trial and error, mistakes, embarrassments, sweating, sleepless nights, and a lot of practicing.

Overcoming any fear will take baby steps at first, but with a good plan the fear can be overcome. Some steps may be:

1. Put yourself in the listener's position and ask what a listener expects from a good speaker.
2. Listen to good speakers, and ask why their speeches were so good? Take notes.
3. Ask yourself what the message is that you want to convey to the listener.
4. If you want to teach something, you must know the learning styles of the listeners. If they are visual, have pictures, props, and other training aids for them to see. If they learn best by reading, then have material, online and in hard copy, for them

160

to study. There is more than one way to learn, so you must teach in more than one style or 75% of your students will be bored and lost.

5. Of course, you must write the speech and practice the speech out loud. Make sure it flows well so that you do not get tongue-tied. Rewrite the speech and practice it again, if necessary. Check it for length.

6. Start small—give a one-minute speech in front of people, work up to a five-minute speech, then to 30 minutes, and then to one hour. Gain confidence and keep reading books on speaking in public and get better. Confidence will come in time, and the fear will go away. The first five minutes are the worst. Your body is sweating, you are breathing fast, it is difficult to smile, and you are not sure if you want to stay or run. But you cannot hold on to the fear when your mind does not perceive any danger, and the body will slowly stop the fear process. Once you have made it past the five-minute mark things will become better, easier, and start to flow.

7. Many people quit before they see any real progress, or they stop learning new techniques. You must practice new things, like walking around the stage and getting away from the podium, expanding your knowledge of the subject matter, and learning how to more effectively engage the audience.

The fear of public speaking can be overcome by the desire to do it, the proper training, and practice, practice, practice. Once you experience a good speech, feel confident, and get congratulated for a good speech, the fear will start to decrease and the love will increase. Sometimes the love will push the fear away. The key is to practice, practice, and then practice some more.

Dale Carnegie has a list of things to do for public speaking in "How to Make Rapid and Easy Progress in Learning to Speak in Public"

According to Carnegie, you should speak about something that:

- You have earned the right to talk about through study and experience;
- You are excited about; and
- You are eager to tell your listeners about.

He counsels as follows:

- Make brief notes of the interesting things you want to mention.
- Don't write out your talks.
- Never, never, never memorize a talk word for word.
- Fill your talk with illustrations and examples.
- Know far more about your subject than you can use.
- Rehearse your talk by conversing with your friends.
- Instead of worrying about your delivery, find ways of improving it.
- Don't imitate others; be yourself.

CHAPTER 19

QUOTES ON FEAR

"I am convinced that life is 10% what happens to me and 90% how I react to it." – Charles R. Swindoll

"The message is clear. It is not what is happening 'out there.' It is what is happening between your ears. It's your attitude that counts. Get your attitude right, and chances are dramatically higher that your economic condition will be good." – Zig Ziglar

"If you change the way you look at things, the things you look at change." – Dr. Wayne Dyer

"It is not what happens to you but how you think about what happens to you that determines how you feel and react. It is not the world outside of you that dictates your circumstances or conditions. It is the world inside you that creates the conditions of your life." – Brian Tracy

"I used to say, 'I sure hope things will change.' Then I learned that the only way things are going to change for me is when I change." – Jim Rohn

"The great breakthrough in your life comes when you realize that you can learn anything you need to learn to accomplish any goal that you set for yourself. This means there are no limits on what you can be, have, or do." – Brian Tracy

"You cannot change your destination overnight, but you can change your direction overnight." – Jim Rohn

Courage

"All that you accomplish or fail to accomplish with your life is the direct result of your thoughts." – James Allen

"Whether you be man or woman you will never do anything in this world without courage. It is the greatest quality of the mind next to honor." – James Allen

"There is a time to take counsel of your fears, and there is a time to never listen to any fear." – George S. Patton

"One of the greatest discoveries a man makes, one of his great surprises, is to find he can do what he was afraid he couldn't do." – Henry Ford

"He who would accomplish little must sacrifice little; he who would achieve much must sacrifice much; he who would attain highly must sacrifice greatly." – James Allen

"Pain is weakness leaving the body." – Navy Diving Instructors

"Courage is not the absence of fear, it's the mastery of it." – Zig Ziglar

"Courage is not the only virtue but the form of every virtue at the testing point." – C. S. Lewis

"You have to find something that you love enough to be able to take risks, jump over the hurdles and break through the brick walls that are always going to be placed in front of you. If you don't have that kind of

feeling for what it is you're doing, you'll stop at the first giant hurdle."
– George Lucas

"People think I'm disciplined. It is not discipline. It is devotion. There is a great difference." – Luciano Pavarotti

"Never talk defeat. Use words like hope, belief, faith, victory." – Norman Vincent Peale

"My mentor said, 'Let's go do it,' not 'You go do it.' How powerful when someone says, 'Let's!'" – Jim Rohn

"A lot of people have gone farther than they thought they could because someone else thought they could." – Zig Ziglar

"Love to be real, it must cost—it must hurt—it must empty us of self." – Mother Teresa

"It is not what we do that makes us holy, but the love with which we do it." – St. Thérèse de Lisieux

"Ladies and Gentlemen, It takes guts, it is rough, it's not easy, when you question yourself, Can I do this? When you got to be your own boss and have to work for yourself. People will think you are crazy and you will think you are crazy. When everything and everyone is against you…remember it's not over till you win. – Les Brown

"Never, never, never give up." – Winston Churchill

"Courage is not the absence of fear; it is the conquest of it."– Anonymous

"He who loses wealth loses much; he who loses a friend loses more; but he that loses courage loses all." – Miguel de Cervantes

"Courage is doing what you're afraid to do. There can be no courage unless you're scared." – Eddie Rickenbacker

"I count him braver who overcomes his desires than him who conquers his enemies, for the hardest victory is over self."– Aristotle

"Courage is not the absence of fear, but rather the judgment that something else is more important than fear." – Ambrose Redmoon Fear

"The history of the human race is the history of ordinary people who have overcome their fears and accomplished extraordinary things." – Brian Tracy

"The first time that I appeared on stage, it scared me to death. I really didn't know what all the yelling was about. I didn't realize that my body was moving. It's a natural thing to me." – Elvis Presley

"Inaction breeds doubt and fear. Action breeds confidence and courage. If you want to conquer fear, do not sit home and think about it. Go out and get busy." – Dale Carnegie

"Fear makes come true, that which one is afraid of." – Victor Frankl

"Our doubts are traitors and make us lose the good we oft might win, by fearing to attempt." – William Shakespeare

"Consult not your fears but your hopes and your dreams. Think not about your frustrations, but about your unfulfilled potential. Concern yourself not with what you tried and failed in, but with what it is still possible for you to do." – Pope John XXIII

"Anything I've ever done that ultimately was worthwhile initially scared me to death." – Betty Bender

"The fear, is worse than the pain." – Shannon Bahr

"Fear is the main source of superstition, and one of the main sources of cruelty. To conquer fear is the beginning of wisdom." – Bertrand Russell

"You don't face your fears, you stand up to them." – Anonymous

"Courage is not the absence of fear, but rather the judgment that something else is more important than fear." – Ambrose Redmoon

"Each time we face our fear, we gain strength, courage, and confidence in the doing." – Theodore Roosevelt

"No passion so effectually robs the mind of all its powers of acting and reasoning as fear." – Edmund Burke

"You gain strength, courage, and confidence by every experience in which you really stop to look fear in the face. You must do the thing which you think you cannot do."– Eleanor Roosevelt

"The only thing we have to fear is fear itself." – Franklin D. Roosevelt

"The team that won't be beat, can't be beat." – Knute Rockne

"I have learned over the years that when one's mind is made up, this diminishes fear; knowing what must be done does away with fear." – Rosa Parks

"The little me on the outside is strangling the Big me on the inside." – Enrico Caruso

"Everything can be taken from a man but one thing: the last of the human freedoms—to choose one's attitude in any given set of circumstances, to choose one's own way." – Victor Frankl

"Avoiding danger is no safer in the long run than outright exposure. The fearful are caught as often as the bold." – Helen Keller

"A coward dies a thousand deaths, but the valiant taste death but once." The actual quote is from Act 1, Scene 2, Line 32 of *Julius Caesar* by William Shakespeare.

"Where fear is present, wisdom cannot be." – Lactantius

"No passion so effectually robs the mind of all its powers of acting and reasoning as fear." - Edmund Burke

"If a man harbors any sort of fear, it percolates through all his thinking, damages his personality, makes him landlord to a ghost." – Lloyd Cassel Douglas

"Fear has its use, but cowardice has none. I may not put my hand into the jaws of a snake, but the very sight of the snake need not strike terror into me. The trouble is that we often die many times before death overtakes us." – Mahatma Gandhi

"Never let the fear of striking out get in your way." – Babe Ruth

"The greatest mistake you can make in life is to be continually fearing that you will make one." – Elbert Hubbard

"Fear makes come true that which one is afraid of." – Victor Frankl

"You gain strength, courage and confidence by every experience in which you really stop to look fear in the face. You are able to say to yourself. 'I lived through this horror. I can take the next thing that comes along.'" – Eleanor Roosevelt, *You Learn By Living*, 1960

"It was a high counsel that I once heard given to a young person, "Always do what you are afraid to do." – Ralph Waldo Emerson

"I don't fear failure. I only fear the slowing up of the engine inside of me which is pounding, saying, "Keep going, someone must be on top, why not you?" – General George S. Patton

"FEAR is an acronym in the English language for 'False Evidence Appearing Real.'" – Neale Donald Walsh

"Every decision you make—every decision—is not a decision about what to do. It's a decision about Who You Are. When you see this, when you understand it, everything changes. You begin to see life in a new way. All events, occurrences, and situations turn into opportunities to do what you came here to do." – Neale Donald Walsh

I must not fear.
Fear is the mind-killer.
Fear is the little-death that brings total obliteration.
I will face my fear.
I will permit it to pass over me and through me.
And when it has gone past I will turn the inner eye to see its path.
Where the fear has gone there will be nothing.
Only I will remain.

– Frank Herbert

Overcoming Obstacles

"We all have dreams, but in order to make dreams into reality, it takes an awful lot of determination, dedication, self-discipline and effort." – Jesse Owens

"Gold medals aren't really made of gold. They're made of sweat, determination, and a hard-to-find alloy called guts." – Dan Gable

"I've always found that anything worth achieving will always have obstacles in the way and you've got to have that drive and determination to overcome those obstacles en route to whatever it is that you want to accomplish." – Chuck Norris

"The bravest sight in the world is to see a great man struggling against adversity." – Lucius Annaeus Seneca

"We generally change ourselves for one of two reasons: inspiration or desperation." – Jim Rohn

"A man has to learn that he cannot command things, but that he can command himself; that he cannot coerce the wills of others, but that he can mold and master his own will: and things serve him who serves Truth; people seek guidance of him who is master of himself." – James Allen

CHAPTER 20

RECOMMENDED READING

Man of Steel and Velvet – Aubrey Andelin

How to Stop Worrying and Start Living – Dale Carnegie

Think and Grow Rich – Napoleon Hill

The Millionaire Next Door – Stanley/Danko

The 4-hour Workweek – Timothy Ferriss

The Richest Man in Babylon – George S. Clason

Leadership 101 – John Maxwell

Man's Search for Meaning – Victor Frankl

Life is an Attitude: A Tragedy Turns to Triumph – Ron Heagy/Donita Dyer

How to Win Friends and Influence People – Dale Carnegie

The Art of Public Speaking – Dale Carnegie

Sales Dogs – Blair Singer

About the Author

David Doctor is a retired U.S. Navy Chief and Explosive Ordnance Disposal Technician. A graduate of the State University of New York, David lives in Las Cruces, New Mexico, with his wife, Xuhong. He currently travels around the United States working for the U.S. Army Corp of Engineers cleaning up explosives and unexploded ordnance on old bombing ranges.

REFERENCES

Merriam-Webster's Collegiate Dictionary, 11ᵗʰ Edition, http://www. merriam-webster.com/.

How Stuff Works, http://science.howstuffworks.com/life/fear.htm – *fear response in the brain.*

Naval Diving and Salvage, http://www.navy.com/careers/special-operations/diver.html.

Norman Vincent Peale, *Help Yourself with God's Help*, Chapter 8, "How to Get Rid of Fear," http://www.guidepostsfoundation.org/files-gpf/ Help%20Yourself.pdf.

Dale Carnegie, "How to Make Rapid and Easy Progress in Learning to Speak in Public" in *Speak More Effectively,* Dale Carnegie, available at http://sales.dalecarnegie.com/general/files/website/ SpeakingEffectively.pdf.

CPSIA information can be obtained at www.ICGtesting.com
Printed in the USA
LVOW08s0541241213

366602LV00004B/305/P